Filter Shift

How Effective People
***SEE** the World*

SARA TAYLOR

NEW YORK

NASHVILLE   MELBOURNE

Filter Shift
*How Effective People **SEE** the World*

Published in New York, New York, by Morgan James Publishing. Morgan James and The Entrepreneurial Publisher are trademarks of Morgan James, LLC. www.MorganJamesPublishing.com

The Morgan James Speakers Group can bring authors to your live event. For more information or to book an event visit The Morgan James Speakers Group at www.TheMorganJamesSpeakersGroup.com.

ISBN 978-1-63047-978-7 paperback
ISBN 978-1-63047-979-4 eBook
Library of Congress Control Number: 2016902474

Shelfie

A **free** eBook edition is available with the purchase of this print book.

CLEARLY PRINT YOUR NAME ABOVE IN UPPER CASE

Instructions to claim your free eBook edition:
1. Download the Shelfie app for Android or iOS
2. Write your name in **UPPER CASE** above
3. Use the Shelfie app to submit a photo
4. Download your eBook to any device

Cover Design by:
Chris Treccani
www.3dogdesign.net

Interior Design by:
Bonnie Bushman
The Whole Caboodle Graphic Design

Morgan James
The Entrepreneurial Publisher™

Builds

with...

Habitat for Humanity®
Peninsula and Greater Williamsburg

In an effort to support local communities, raise awareness and funds, Morgan James Publishing donates a percentage of all book sales for the life of each book to Habitat for Humanity Peninsula and Greater Williamsburg.

Get involved today! Visit
www.MorganJamesBuilds.com

Filter Shift®

Contents

Foreword

By Joel Comm

New York Times Bestselling Author,
Futurist, and Professional Speaker

Prejudice. It's a word that instantly triggers something in each of us. On one hand we are appalled when someone expresses prejudice against another, whether it be based on race, religion, gender, sexuality, or appearance.

On the other hand, if we are honest with ourselves, we cringe a little or a lot when our own prejudices come into play.

The bottom line is that no one likes to be judged. The preconceived notions others have about us are usually incorrect, if not way off. It stands to reason that our ideas about others often miss the mark as well. How many times have you said, "I thought X would be like this, but once I got to know her I found she wasn't like that at all"?

The problem is that we all do it—we all "pre-judge" the actions and beliefs of other people. Our brains are hardwired for it. So does that mean we're all bad?

Well, I won't answer for you, but I'm pretty sure I have at least a few redeeming qualities. If that's true for you and (I'll make a leap) lots of other people out there too, what do we do with this knowledge? How do we avoid doing something our brains are built to do? Thankfully, according to Sara Taylor, we don't have to.

The difference in her thinking, as outlined in this book, is that no, we can't stop the process of reacting to people and situations with (let's be honest) all our prejudices showing; however, what we can do is build up a solid understanding of *why we react to any given person or situation with particular prejudices in the first place.* Go back and read that sentence again—it's important.

The key is in the title of this book: *Filter Shift*™. Our prejudices are like filters that drop down between *actual* perception (what we experience) and the attempt to *understand* what we experienced. The filter "colors our view," you could say. And once we start recognizing the filters we use to understand any given situation, we can start making choices about whether or not a particular filter will be useful, whether or not it will help us communicate with other living, breathing human beings.

It's said that the goal of all communication is understanding. And it is these filters in our unconscious mind that become stumbling blocks to understanding others for who they really are.

What are the filters that get in the way of creating and nurturing healthy and prosperous relationships, both personally and in business? How can we become fully aware of the filters and be able to spot when our own bias is getting in the way? How may we be equipped to take control of our biases so our best intentions result in manifesting a positive impact in all we do?

The end-goal here is *more effective communication*: across race, across generations, across genders, across religious beliefs and sexual orientation and political ideology. And that's only the tip of the proverbial iceberg. The implications of this line of thought are immense, in business, politics, human rights and social justice, education, medicine, policing—anywhere people need to communicate effectively with one another.

So quit listening to me and start reading. I can't promise learning to Filter Shift™ is going to be easy, but Sara will walk you through it one step at a time. And you may well find, in time, that it's the most valuable skill you ever learned.

Introduction

Springing up like a mirage from the sand, the ornate palace was an eerie site for Bill Richardson. After traveling for days across a barren desert, he now entered the opulent domain of a dictator. Its expansive yet empty rooms exuded power with their shiny marble floors, thick gold-accented columns, and canopies of colorful baroque ceilings. It was the palace of Saddam Hussein—lavish even by dictator standards. Richardson and his team of three other US emissaries were ushered in past a display of military sentries and led to the meeting room lined with Hussein's revolutionary guards in crisp, bright uniforms, gripping their shiny gold swords.

This meeting was the result of three months of stressful negotiations with the Iraqis, and intense planning and preparation by the US team. Richardson, among other things, was the former governor of New Mexico and former ambassador to the UN. It was during this, one of the earliest skirmishes with Iraq, that President Clinton had sent him to negotiate with Hussein.

Yet, only minutes after arriving, Hussein abruptly left and the meeting was terminated. Richardson sat stunned. As he heard Hussein slam the door behind him, he could feel the table still vibrating from the pounding of the dictator's fist. Hussein's chair on the other side swiveled in slow circles from the sudden abandonment of its owner.

Richardson was both baffled by what had gone wrong and worried for his safety, as eight towering Republican Guards surrounded him. It suddenly didn't matter that he and his team had prepared for months. It didn't matter that he had positive intent, or that he sincerely wanted to connect with Hussein to negotiate. What did matter was that he had somehow offended Hussein.

How did months of effort and hard work come to nothing after only a few short moments? How could such an accomplished leader as Bill Richardson so visibly and suddenly fail? Because he had blind spots. Because he was unable to *Filter Shift*: to see his own filters, understand the filters of Saddam Hussein, and shift his behavior when the situation called for it.[1]

---

1   Governor Bill Richardson, *How to Sweet-Talk a Shark: Strategies and Stories from a Master Negotiator* (Rodale, 2013).

Chapter One

Of Dictators, Blind Spots, and Personal Effectiveness

S o what exactly happened to end the meeting between Saddam Hussein and Bill Richardson before it even began? Unconsciously filtering the situation to believe that he could be informal, Richardson settled in when he sat down for the meeting. Angled in his chair, leaning with one arm over the back, he crossed his ankle over his knee, his flexed foot pointing the bottom of his shoe toward Hussein. That was the moment Hussein pounded the table and terminated the meeting, leaving the US team baffled.

What Richardson didn't know was that, in many Arab countries, showing the sole of your shoe is a blatant symbol of disrespect. The equivalent of this act in the United States would be an Iraqi emissary meeting with President Clinton, walking into the oval office, calmly sitting down, and flipping Clinton the bird, both middle fingers proudly raised. Just look at pictures of the Arab Spring uprisings of protests that began in 2010 throughout the League of Arab States and the surrounding areas. Image after image shows protestors in the streets screaming their disgust and waving the *soles of their shoes* at placards of their rulers.

By crossing his legs, he unwittingly revealed the sole of his shoe to Hussein—a gesture so obvious to those Richardson came to meet with, yet missed by him in his inability to Filter Shift.

Fortunately for Richardson, his inability to Filter Shift wasn't fatal. It caused delays and unnecessary tension, but finally, after stressful re-negotiations, the meeting was resumed and he left having accomplished his objectives, though still unclear as to how he initially sent the meeting off in the wrong direction.

Richardson isn't alone. In fact, the vast majority of us aren't cognizant of how our filters control our thoughts, behaviors, and decisions. Unlike Richardson, our meetings are with coworkers, not dictators. Yet very much like Richardson, in those meetings our filters can misguide us.

At times, as with Richardson, our filters lead to failure for us. There are the more obvious failures: the leader whose speech to the company nosedives, the extensive marketing campaign

> ...the vast majority of us aren't cognizant of how our filters control our thoughts, behaviors, and decisions.

that fails, and the merger that flops. Each failure is preceded by extensive preparation resulting in a naive confidence in the ability to perform, and followed by confusion at the unexplained source of the failure.

In these cases, the results of automatic filtering are obvious. More frequently, however, our individual failures or mishaps caused by an inability to Filter Shift aren't on such a grand scale and are therefore much less obvious. They happen on a day-by-day, moment-by-moment basis, and we're blind to the full spectrum of perception and belief at play, oblivious to our ineffectiveness. We leave a conversation or situation and we think we've communicated successfully, yet we haven't; we think we're effective, yet we aren't. We have significant blind spots that leave us drastically overestimating our effectiveness.

To complicate things, when it comes to *difference*, we typically see only a very narrow spectrum of variables. Things that are "easier" to recognize like gender, race, and language, we see easily enough; however, while those differences are frequently important, they're only part of a much broader spectrum of differences that tend to be outside of our awareness. When misunderstandings or conflicts arise, more often than not they are caused by the differences that we don't see—differences obscured by our automatic filters.

Without the ability to Filter Shift, we can see very little of the full complexity of differences at play, and thus frequently misattribute misunderstandings to those few things that are in our immediate awareness, furthering the misunderstanding (see fig. 1.1).

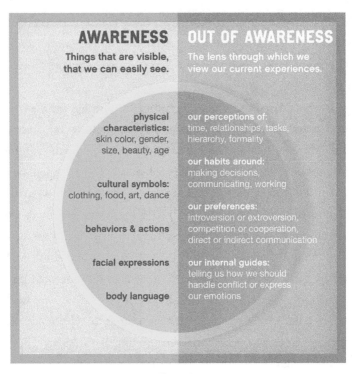

Figure 1.1. We typically see a very narrow spectrum of difference. Only when we learn to Filter Shift can we see the full spectrum of differences.

So what can we do about this problem with our individual and collective vision? If automatic filtering of experiences is hardwired into our brains, is there anything we *can* do about it? How could so many of us not only be ineffective, but also unaware of that ineffectiveness? Put plainly, we just haven't been taught anything different. We actually don't know any better. And when the vast majority of people around us are stuck in the same cycle of automatic filtering, we not only don't see a need for anything different, we also *reinforce* that filtering for each other.

False Prescriptions

When it comes to our interactions across difference—frankly, all interactions—an unconscious optometrist chooses our filters based on *false prescriptions* we write for ourselves. This process is completely natural; our brains are wired to react this way. Our perception of any given situation is filtered quickly and unconsciously. We don't even realize a filter through which to view an interaction has been preselected without our conscious participation. These false prescriptions are rooted in our misconceptions of our own cultural competence. Recognizing them for what they are is an essential first step in learning to Filter Shift.

Prescription #1: I'm not around people who are different from me that much, so it's a moot point.

Every interaction is an interaction across difference. That means we all experience this, all the time. I'm misled if I think this person is just like me because I don't see any obvious differences between the two of us—we're the same race, gender, age, etc. Yet we are different because our filters are different, and it is our filters that determine how we see and respond to each other. If we allow ourselves to be lulled by external similarities, we easily miss the broader spectrum.

Prescription #2: Exposure = Competence

Here we make statements like "I'm around differences all the time. I have a gay couple for neighbors, my mom has lived with a disability all my life, and my best friend is black!" The inherent belief in these statements is that "I am exposed to difference, therefore I am competent in my interactions across difference"—as if a new skillset is in the air when differences are present and all we need to do is breathe it in. The ability to interact effectively across difference, like any other complex skill, needs to be consciously developed. Think of it in comparison to developing math skills. You would never assume a child could learn math if you just sat them in a room all day where mathematicians were present. As with math, we need intentional, developmental learning and practice to nurture this skill.

Prescription #3: I get this stuff; it's my coworkers (or spouse or neighbors) that don't!

Most people, if asked, would say that they do pretty well interacting across difference—that they are already fairly competent. Yet the reality is that only a very small percentage of us actually *are* competent. This ever-present gap between our perception and reality leads to much of the confusion and conflict that happens as we interact across difference. If I believe I "get it" and still experience situations where interactions with others are ineffective, then it must be *their* issue.

Prescription #4: Identity = Competence

This prescription is particularly tricky in that, while widely believed, it goes unspoken more often than not. It's the notion that people from marginalized groups—especially people of color and women—are somehow more skilled at interacting across difference, that somehow the experiences tied to our identity inherently increase the reality of our perceptions. In actuality, that's simply not the case. Going back to the second prescription, we need to deliberately develop the ability to Filter Shift, no matter our cultural origins or identity.

Prescription #5: I'm colorblind!

This comment is typically heard as an individual is trying to frame him/herself as a generally good person. The assumption is that only *bad* people have biases while in actuality we *all* have biases. Biases are morality-neutral. They're a natural product of our brains working to categorize and make sense of the world for us. Eliminating bias is an unattainable goal. Instead, to be more effective, we need to recognize and understand our biases and their impact on how we see and operate. We can only do that by acknowledging that we have biases in the first place.

Prescription #6: Comfort = Competence

We've all felt discomfort at one point or another in our lives as we have encountered difference. It may have been the first time we ate dinner at a friend's house, or the first time we walked into a new workplace, new neighborhood, or new country. The fallacy here comes when we believe that as the discomfort dissipates, a generalized competence somehow materializes. However, just because we've become comfortable in a particular situation, or with a particular person, doesn't mean we've learned how to be effective outside of that single situation or with anyone other than that particular individual.

Learning to Filter Shift

Our unconscious mind snaps filters into place so fast it feels natural to see things the way we do. The judgments we make (based on what we see) feel "right," "correct," "good," "obvious." However, as demonstrated above, we're not seeing clearly. Our automatic filters are limiting the spectrum of difference we perceive while presenting the illusion of clarity. At first glance this problem can seem overwhelming. I mean, what can we possibly do about a process we don't consciously perceive happening? How do we see beyond these false prescriptions?

The answer is surprisingly simple—though please note I said simple, not easy. We learn how to *Filter Shift*. Filter Shifting is the ability to SEE Self, SEE Others, and SEE an effective approach. We train ourselves first to clearly see our own filters, then to recognize the situations in which they're likely to be used, and

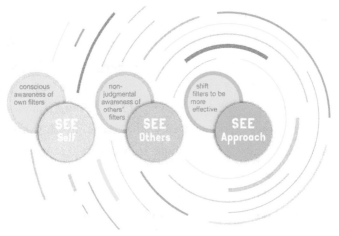

Figure 1.2. Filter Shift: SEE Self, SEE Others, SEE Approach

finally, to *consciously shift those filters*, opening our eyes bit by bit to the whole available spectrum of difference (see fig. 1.2). When we're aware of how our unconscious mind filters and decides things for us, then we can also begin to see the complexity of filters that are at play in the unconscious minds of those with whom we are interacting, and respond effectively to the richness of that complexity.

SEE Self, SEE Others, SEE Approach. You may have noticed the capital letters of SEE in the Filter Shift steps. That's not just because I like the word *see*—which I do—or because what we see and pay attention to is important as we learn to

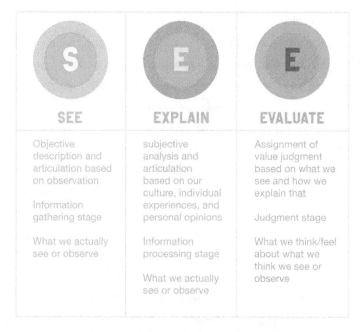

SEE	EXPLAIN	EVALUATE
Objective description and articulation based on observation	subjective analysis and articulation based on our culture, individual experiences, and personal opinions	Assignment of value judgment based on what we see and how we explain that
Information gathering stage	Information processing stage	Judgment stage
What we actually see or observe	What we actually see or observe	What we think/feel about what we think we see or observe

Figure 1.3. SEE helps us understand our three levels of observation: See, Explain, and Evaluate.

Filter Shift—which it is. SEE is actually an acronym for *See*, *Explain*, and *Evaluate* (see fig. 1.3). We'll discuss this further in chapter eight.

Think Wine

To better understand this ability to Filter Shift, I like to use wine as an analogy—specifically, our ability to distinguish differences in wine. While I enjoy a good glass of wine, I'm certainly no connoisseur. I do better than some people who can only distinguish three different kinds of wine—red, white, and pink. Since I like dry, full-bodied wine, I can pick out those traits, but put a Shiraz and a Cabernet in front of me and I wouldn't know which is which.

There are those who could tell you not only which is the Cabernet, but also which Cabernet is Chilean or Spanish. Then there are the sommeliers who can distinguish not only that a particular wine is Spanish, but also the vintage of the wine, the specific vineyard it came from, and even if it came from grapes grown on a hill versus in a valley—that's quite a bit more complexity than just red, white, and pink.

The small percentage of individuals who are able to Filter Shift can see the same level of complexity, but in their interactions with others. Like the sommeliers, they experience richness in the complexity of the available spectrum of differences.

Is the sommelier a better person because they experience that richness? Would we say they are *good* and the neophyte of wine is *bad*? No. They just have different levels of competence. It's not a reflection of who they are as people; it's what they are capable of when it comes to wine.

The same is true for the competence of interacting across difference. Those with a lesser ability aren't bad, while those with a greater ability are good. It's just a reflection of their capability in distinguishing and responding to differences. Can we increase those capabilities? Yes. Whether discerning differences in wine or in people, capability can be developed.

Only a small percentage of people—those who work in a liquor store or a fine-dining establishment—need the skills of the sommelier. But the skill of being able to identify, understand, and interact effectively across differences in people? Bill Richardson isn't the only one who would have benefited from it. Since that ability comes into play in every interaction, it's critical for every one of us, every day. This book is about that ability and how any of us can develop it.

• • • Key Points • • •

- The vast majority of us don't realize how our automatic filters control our thoughts, behaviors, and decisions.
- An inability to Filter Shift can cause grand-scale failures but typically results in mishaps and misunderstandings that are much less obvious. They happen on a day-by-day, moment-by-moment basis. Most of the time we're blind to them, oblivious to our ineffectiveness.
- When it comes to difference, we have a very small spectrum of what is typically in our awareness, and a much larger spectrum of differences that tend to be out of our awareness.
- The reason so many of us are ineffective in our interactions across difference is that we have yet to be taught how to

operate differently. We also perpetuate that ineffectiveness with each other. One way we do that is by writing false prescriptions for ourselves.

- Filter Shifting is the ability to SEE Self, SEE Others, SEE Approach. It allows us to see the complexity of filters that are at play in the unconscious mind—both our own filters and the filters of others—and then respond competently to that complexity.
- The SEE in each step is our levels of observation: See, Explain, Evaluate.

Chapter Two

A SEEing Problem

I'm Proud to Say I'm Colorblind

The enthusiasm visibly drained from Jordan's face, taken over by disbelief, then anger, when he heard his leader pronounce, "I'm proud to say I'm colorblind. I treat all my staff equally—black, white, or purple; I see everyone the same." As the only person of color on the team, Jordan suddenly felt exposed, his difference called out yet dismissed at the same time. Annoyance mixed with fury washed over him. All he could think was, "Why would you not want to see color? Why would that be something to be proud of?" There was an underlying belief to this declaration of colorblindness: that color must somehow be *bad*.

This situation plays out in our interactions more often than we'd like to admit. It might be from the "colorblind" leader or it might be when the one baby boomer joining the team of millennials is told, "You know, you don't feel like you're my grandpa; you actually feel like one of us!" In each of these cases, the intent is positive and the desire is to include. Unfortunately, that positive intent is not always matched with an equally positive impact.

> In each of these cases, the intent is positive and the desire is to include. Unfortunately, that positive intent is not always matched with an equally positive impact.

A participant in one of my trainings once shared a great example of this dynamic from a clip of a reality TV show. In it, an obese woman described herself as fat, and when the man she was with countered and said, "No, you're not fat," she exploded. "How can you say I'm not fat when I clearly am? Just the fact that you say I'm not means you actually think fat is bad and ugly; otherwise you'd be able to say that I'm fat, if you didn't think fat is ugly."

You're Just Like One of the Guys

I experienced this SEEing problem myself early in my career. "We love working with you, Sara, because you're just like one of the guys!" I heard that comment frequently when I was working with a group of construction company owners. Just by that description and their comment to me, you can probably guess the demographics of that group.

Yes, they were all men.

I was leading Diversity and Inclusion work for a large county government. One of my responsibilities was to initiate a Supplier Diversity program. Since the most significant dollars spent by the county were on construction contracts, one of my stakeholder groups was comprised of the construction company owners that had received most of the county contracts in the past. We met frequently, and on several occasions I was slapped on the back and told, in one form or another, "Sara, it's so great to work with you because you're just like one of the guys."

Yet it was clear to me that I wasn't. I was an outsider. I was left out of emails, meetings were scheduled without my knowing, any idea I presented wasn't an idea until it came from one of them, and decisions were made without me. I was *clearly* not one of them. Yet somehow they didn't see this. In their eyes, their intent and its impact on me were the same.

In response to a situation like this, particularly if it's persistent, few are able to remain positive, strategize a response, and be productive. More typically, the response is fight or flight.

I'm not proud to admit that when I faced the construction company owners, flight was my response. That's not to say I actually left the group—I have a strong sense of responsibility and so I kept showing up, but only physically. I was young, inexperienced, and baffled by the situation. I essentially froze. Engagement? Contribution? Nope. I think I just "got by."

I didn't choose the fight option, but many others do because that's also a natural response. If we are told over and over again that others don't see a critical part of our identity, then we start to show them that identity, even shove it in their faces, because we *want to be seen clearly*. In my case, that would have looked like me showing up in a T-shirt emblazoned with "I Am Woman Hear Me Roar" and drinking from a "Woman Power" coffee cup. I'd have come to a meeting with the construction company owners and announced I was using funds from the group to go to a National Empowerment of Women conference. And, of course, I'd also go into detail about the keynote topic, "How to Deal with the Male Chauvinist Pigs of the Workplace."

I'm exaggerating in my example, yet this is an accurate reflection of the dynamic. Typically with positive intentions, thinking it's seeing clearly, a majority group turns a blind eye to the differences of a minority group. And when those differences are tied to identity, the responses span the spectrum from confusion, frustration, defensiveness, and anger to even guilt and eventual self-hatred.

The Golden...Filter?

Growing up, many of us learned and perhaps even still try to live by what's commonly known as the Golden Rule: "Do unto others as you would have them do unto you." This is a wonderful premise that teaches us the basic principles of thinking of others and being respectful.

Unfortunately, this rule is often the beginning of our larger SEEing problem.

For many of us, the Golden Rule feels like a *universal* rule—something you could apply in any situation and expect a positive outcome. It feels this way because of our underlying unconscious assumption that any given person is essentially *just like us*. This assumption of similarity, believing that everyone sees the world the way we do, is what actually *lessens* the rule's viability as a guide for our behavior. This is what convinced Jordan's boss that he could be "colorblind" in the first place; this is what convinced the guys I worked with that, well, I *wanted* to be "one of the guys."

Bill Richardson learned the ineffectiveness of the Golden Rule the hard way. Being informal and taking an informal posture as they began the tense negotiations is likely what he would have wanted had he been in Saddam Hussein's position.

That kind of thinking—*what would I want if I were in their shoes?*—is essentially the Golden Rule, and it overlooks differences. It assumes that what Richardson would want if he were in Hussein's position is the same as what Hussein might want. Richardson processed the situation through his own automatic filters, assuming that how he saw the situation was the same as how Hussein would see it—and we know how making that assumption turned out for Richardson!

If the alternative is to be unkind to others, then yes, this rule seems to be an unambiguously clear choice for guiding our behavior. But there is another alternative that is even more effective—the *Platinum Rule*, which is to treat others as they would like to be treated. This rule requires us to be fully aware of, and responsively adaptive to, differences. This option is where we can be our most effective. It is where we are able to see the full complexity of differences that

> This rule requires us to be fully aware of, and responsively adaptive to, differences. This option is where we can be our most effective. It is where we are able to see the full complexity of differences that others bring, not simply judge based on our own bias.

others bring, not simply judge based on our own bias. We then adjust our response directly to those differences.

This opportunity becomes available to us when we are fully aware of others' filters and are able to Filter Shift.

Universal Values

Typically when we apply the Golden Rule, we're thinking about *universal values*. Anne Frank wrote, "We all live with the objective of being happy: our lives are all different and yet the same."[2] We see through a lens that covers us all in the same golden light. And the tricky thing is, it's even true to a certain extent. We know that across the world, regardless of race, religion, or geography, most peoples and cultures hold certain values as positive—truth, love, and loyalty, as examples.

Yet the way we *display* those values can be very different. This is because the groups we are a part of believe they are creating a *shared meaning* of *universal values*. However, what's really happening is that we are agreeing on a *standard perception* of *particular behaviors*. And the kicker here? Again, this whole process is completely natural; our brains are wired to react this way. Because our perception of any given situation is filtered so quickly, even unconsciously, we don't even realize that this connection has been made. We rarely stop to think that someone else, from a different group with different filters, might attach a very different value to the same behavior. Our groups decide how we exhibit the value in question or, in other words, the behaviors we will identify with the value.

---

2   Anne Frank, *Anne Frank: The Diary of a Young Girl* (Bantam, 1993).

Our groups also decide how we will prioritize values. A group that prioritizes honesty over respect may automatically filter that value, seeing *direct* communication as *honest* communication, and placing that first in importance. Ask a colleague with this filter what they think about your work product and they'll likely tell you very specifically, good or bad, assuming that's what you want them to do. And you'd rather they be *honest* than hold back out of *respect*.

Conversely, a group that prioritizes respect over honesty may automatically filter that value, seeing *indirect* communication as more *respectful* communication, and placing it first in importance. A colleague with this filter may not tell you in a straightforward way what they think about your work, but will find another way to answer your question, assuming you'd feel disrespected if they did otherwise; and you'd rather they be *respectful* (especially if you're their supervisor or manager) than directly *honest*.

Both groups value honesty and respect; however, the automatic filters that drop in place in a situation where these values are relevant will cause both to see the *same behavior* differently, depending on how it lines up with their *standard perception* of the behavior in question. Where we often run afoul of automatic filtering is when we assume that any universal value will be universally understood: "At XYZ Company, we value a respectful workplace for all our associates." The following

Both groups value honesty and respect; however, the automatic filters that drop in place in a situation where these values are relevant will cause both to see the *same behavior* differently...

extended example shows us how this positively intended attempt at respect all too often plays out.

She's So Disrespectful!

Let's say I have two staff members, one an extreme introvert, Alicia, the other, Sam, an extreme extrovert. As their leader, I have a commitment to creating a respectful workplace. I also happen to share Sam's preference for extroversion. That means that my automatic filters equate extroversion behaviors with respect. When Sam comes to me to complain about Alicia, naturally he doesn't talk about introversion and extroversion preferences; he talks about respect and productivity—universal values. He also makes the claim that Alicia—and by extension, me, since I'm the leader—is creating a disrespectful workplace with her "unproductive" behavior.

"Our work is so intertwined, it's critical that we know and understand each other well. I try to do that and am constantly reaching out to her. I stop by her office to talk through a problem that I have with my project that I know she may be experiencing too. Since two heads are better than one, I figure if we talk it out, we'll come to a better solution than if I were just sitting at my desk alone trying to figure it out—just common sense, really."

What he's saying makes complete sense to me. As a fellow extrovert, my filters display the situation very similarly to Sam's. When he describes how Alicia responds, I identify with his frustration. "But anytime I do that she's so reluctant. She says she thinks I should just figure it out on my own and she'll do the same, and we can compare notes. What a waste of time! I swear she closes her door when she sees me coming. It's so disrespectful!"

Alarms go off in my head. I'm the leader and there is a suggestion of a disrespectful workplace! Not good. Obviously Alicia, with her disrespectful behavior, is actually inhibiting productivity. I need to get to the bottom of this and maybe even institute some clear policies to avoid having this happen again. My filters don't allow me to see it as an issue of introversion versus extroversion; instead I see it as disrespectful behavior happening right under my nose. It's a mess, and its root cause is a SEEing problem.

Closely examined, the results of automatic filtering can be made pretty obvious. The problem is, scenarios like this happen all the time, and we don't see it. Once again, they occur on a day-by-day, moment-by-moment basis, and we're blind to the full spectrum of perception and belief at play, oblivious to our own ineffectiveness. We leave a conversation or situation and we think we've communicated successfully, yet we haven't; we think we're effective, yet we aren't. We have significant blind spots that leave us drastically overestimating our effectiveness.

● ● ● Key Points ● ● ●

- "I'm colorblind" may be a well-intentioned statement, but saying we don't see obvious physical differences can send a message that the difference is bad.

- Denying obvious differences can lead to the reactions of fight or flight.

- The alternative to the Golden Rule is the Platinum Rule: Treat others as they would like to be treated.

- Universal values don't help us to understand our differences because those values are represented by very different behaviors. We also prioritize those values very differently leading to, again, very different behaviors.

Chapter Three

The Unconscious Optometrist

Our Filters Create Our Reality

n my presentations, I often ask a powerful question that I
first read in *Zero Limits* by Joe Vitale.[3] It's a question that was
posed to him by therapist and healer Ihaleakala Hew Len. Like
Vitale and the hundreds of participants to whom I have raised this
question, I was dumbfounded when I first encountered it.

"Can you tell me what your next thought will be?"

Stop to think about it. Can you?

No. None of us can.

---

3   Joe Vitale, *Zero Limits: The Secret Hawaiian System for Health, Wealth,*
     Peace and More (Wiley, 2007).

How can it be that we don't know what our next thought will be? We don't know because that thought is born in our unconscious mind. Researcher Benjamin Libet of the University of California, San Francisco, and pioneer in the field of the unconscious mind, in his seminal research on the topic identified that our judgments, intentions, and decisions are actually first formulated in our unconscious and only then sent, with full authority and believability, to our conscious.

A fraction of a second before we make a conscious decision, our unconscious has already decided for us. We *think* we are in conscious control and are making our own decisions, when in actuality we aren't; our unconscious is in control and deciding for us. And what does our "unconscious optometrist" prescribe to make those decisions? Filters. In any given situation, thanks to the lightning rearrangement of automatic filters by our unconscious, we immediately end up with what seems to be a very clear, fully formed decision or explanation of reality, and then make the assumption that others have that exact same reality—when of course they don't.

> We *think* we are in conscious control and are making our own decisions, when in actuality we aren't; our unconscious is in control and deciding for us. And what does our "unconscious optometrist" prescribe to make those decisions? Filters.

That's why filters are so powerful, and why it's so vital for us to recognize that power as we learn to Filter Shift.

Let's Start with Intentions

It may be open for debate, but I, at least, have a fundamental belief that the vast majority of us have positive intentions. On a day-by-day, moment-by moment basis, we want to contribute to and have positive experiences with our colleagues, our friends, and our family—in general, with all of those we interact with.

Yet, if that's the case, then why do we have misunderstandings? Why don't we get along and instead end up in conflicts with one another?

Simply put, as we saw in the last chapter, it's because we aren't usually making conscious choices about our reactions to others; instead, an unconscious optometrist is at work, choosing filters for us that cloud our understanding of the impact our behaviors have on others. These filters train our focus only on our *intent*, blinding us to our *impact*.

My Staff Always Loves Me!

That's what happened for Deb. Like most of us, she had positive intent. A successful manager in a small yet dynamic organization, Deb was a very pleasant person, always sincerely cheerful and going out of her way to connect with and listen to her staff. A shock came when she received very negative reviews from the new staff that had just joined her unit as a result of a merger. Her organization had completed a formal evaluation of the merger process, and Deb, along with a few of her fellow managers, had an unsettling wake-up call. She realized that others didn't always experience her positively and that her impact on others didn't match her intent.

"I just don't understand it," she told me during her coaching session. "My staff always loves me! And in this case, I worked for *months* to plan this team merger, continually pushing myself to consider what I would want if I was in their shoes." She had been a successful manager for several years now and was proud of consistently high engagement scores on her team. Her less than stellar impact during this recent merger had shaken her.

"I really do care about my team and wanted to make this a smooth, respectful, and productive process for all the members of my team. No exceptions." She was baffled. How could her hard work and positive intentions not be matched by an equally positive impact?

> Until we've built up our skill in Filter Shifting, we have a very limited ability to predict the impact of our actions, whether they come with a positive intent or not.

Until we've built up our skill in Filter Shifting, we have a very limited ability to predict the impact of our actions, whether they come with a positive intent or not. We also tend to make a significant false assumption, thanks to the filters placed by our friendly unconscious optometrist: that intent equals impact. This is the Golden Filter in all its glory.

I may have the best of intentions when I have a conversation with you, but if I say something that doesn't sit right with you, well, *you* are the one who ultimately decides on the impact of what I've said, not me. I might not mean to hurt you, but if I accidentally step on your toe with my stilettos, you are the one who decides if it was painful or not. That's easier to understand when it's physical pain, but the same concept holds true for emotional pain, or joy for that matter.

The filters used by your unconscious optometrist are formed by your personal experiences. They determine how we perceive raw, experiential information—what we *think* and *feel* about it. Since you obviously haven't all had the same experiences I have, we're not using the same filters, which means you and I perceive the *same information* differently.

One Dog's Bark Is Another Dog's Bite

Carol, a friend of mine, was bitten by a dog when she was little. That experience has stayed with her and influences what she thinks about dogs still today. When she comes to visit me and my big, hyper, yet friendly dog is barking at her, I can't decide for Carol that she understands my dog's friendly intent; her past experiences have prescribed her filters, and that's the starting point of how she'll experience the situation. In this case, having known Carol and her history with dogs for a long time, I can easily understand and empathize with her. I certainly don't take offense that she doesn't want to pet my dog.

Unfortunately, when others experience a negative impact as a result of our actions fueled by positive intent, it's often more difficult for us to understand and empathize. In fact, we much more commonly discount an impact on others when it's the opposite of our intent, either because our own automatic filters blind us to the past experiences related to that feeling, or because we're so focused on our own positive intent that we simply can't connect it to a negative impact.

Mind the Gap

This concept of differing perspectives of intent versus impact has serious implications for our overall individual competence or effectiveness. Let's look at positive intent together with the statistic that we know to be true from the field of cultural competence. The IDI® developed by Mitchell Hammer, PhD, as an assessment that measures specific individual levels of cultural competence, shows us that 95-99 percent of us *significantly overestimate* our cultural competence. That is, we have a significant gap between how effective we *think* we are and how effective we *actually* are.[4] (We'll discuss the IDI model in-depth later in the book.)

So, if my intent is positive—I want, for example, to be respectful and productive—and I also think I'm much more respectful than I actually am, then respect is a skill others need to learn, not me. Bias, of course, is a bad thing. However, since I already "get it," I don't *have* bias. Therefore I don't *need* that diversity training, or that interpersonal relations training, or that cultural competence training. But let me tell you which of my coworkers/supervisors/family members do…

It's Not Just Deb

This brings us to another blind spot: our individual interactions. When we think we are effectively communicating across differences and have a positive intention, if we end up in an interaction that doesn't go well, we typically make two mistakes.

First we assume that even though the interaction didn't go as planned, *we* did what we were supposed to; *we* did the right thing.

---

4   Intercultural Development Inventory®: (Hammer, 1999; Hammer, Bennett & Wiseman, 2003; Hammer, 2007).

Yet the fact that the vast majority of us statistically never see, let alone mind, the perception gap tells us that's likely not the case. And second, we assume negative intent from the other person or people involved. *They* were disrespectful. *They* were unprofessional. *They* don't care about their work, or our relationship, or the future of the organization, or whatever.

However, if we go all the way back to our first assumption at the beginning of this chapter—that they probably had a positive intention, value respect and professionalism, and care about their work as much as we do—then we can see that in actuality the gap between us isn't about respect or any other automatically provided filter, but about an inability to consciously put filters in place that allow our intent and its impact to merge transparently.

Filter Shifting can get us to that place.

Without that ability, we don't even see the complexities that are at play. The result is that we unknowingly cause misunderstandings, even conflict. This was the case for Deb. She had positive intent and worked hard to do her best, but she couldn't see the full spectrum of differences in her new team and therefore wasn't able to effectively respond to them. Fortunately, guiding her to Filter Shift, we were able to help her see the very different perceptions of her new staff and how she had unintentionally caused division. Unfortunately, it came too late as the damage had been done and Deb had more work ahead of her to build trust with her new staff—a challenge she wouldn't have had if she had been able to see the differences when they arose and respond to them in the first place.

And remember, it's not just Deb. The vast majority of us are unable to see the full spectrum of complexities that impact every interaction—a clear view of which our very effectiveness depends on.

That's the bad news.

The good news is that *any* of us can learn to Filter Shift in order to be more effective.

Multiple Valid Realities

Images and thoughts from our past experiences are burned into our filters. Since we don't all have the same past experiences, those images are all different. From the first moment of self-consciousness, our unconscious minds are taking us in different directions. The reality created for each of us is based on these personal images and therefore constantly overlays past experience onto current interaction. In other words, the potential clarity of our automatic filters is obscured by the past; all we end up seeing is *our* self, *our* intentions. The filters are too clouded to let us see anything but the blurriest images of whomever we're interacting with, let alone the actual impact our intentions are having. We believe our intentions to be uncompromised and genuine, even if they aren't. This is why we don't stop to think about others having a different perspective.

At times we do see people acknowledge differing perspectives. At times we do so ourselves. But it's rare and almost always in a situation of conflict when the parties agree to disagree. When I say to you, "I just see this issue differently than you see it," what I'm really saying is, "I see it the right way and you see it the wrong way, and until you see it my way/the right way, we'll just agree to have different perspectives." After all, how can your perspective be right if my very different perspective is also right? And my past experiences confirm it! Unfortunately, yours do the same thing for you. The perspective presented by our individual filters *seems* so real, so correct, it's difficult for us to examine the possibility that there can actually be two (or more!) *equally valid* perspectives and therefore multiple valid realities, all competing to be seen in any given situation.

Keeping all this in mind, it's now time to take a closer look at filters in general.

• • • Key Points • • •

- The vast majority of us have positive intent as we interact with others. Yet we still have misunderstanding and conflict because our filters misinform us and cloud our clear understanding of the impact we have on others.

- Our impact on others determines our effectiveness, not our intent.

- Our filters are formed by our personal experiences. Since our experiences are different, our filters are also different, which leads us to interpret things around us differently.

- According to the IDI®, 95-99 percent of us overestimate how effective we are in our interactions across difference.

- Our unconscious decides for us, and it uses our filters to make those decisions.

- Filter Shifting allows us to merge our intent transparently with the impact we have on others.

Chapter Four

Filters—What We Typically Miss

andy had worked with the developmentally disabled for years, committed to ensuring they had safe environments to live in and were treated with love and care. That love and care were so important to her that it actually made her feel guilty—not guilty that she wasn't doing enough for them, but guilty because she knew that in the back of her mind she held a persistent belief that the developmentally disabled were somehow dirty. She also didn't want to acknowledge that at times she felt afraid they were going to hurt her in some way when working with them. She hated these beliefs and hated herself for having them. Her solution: try not to think about it. Anytime these beliefs popped into her mind, she would shove them back into the recesses hoping they would go away. They didn't.

I met Sandy as a participant in one of my trainings. I had been brought into her organization (a day activity center for the developmentally disabled) to provide unconscious bias training for all of their staff. During the training, I had asked everyone to reflect on an early memory they had of being taught about differences—what their thoughts and feelings were at the time and how it still impacted them today (through an exercise I call "Early Memories." If you'd like to walk through that activity yourself, you can find it here: FilterShift.com/Resources). They each had individual time to write down their reflections and then share those reflections with their small-table groups if they were willing. During that process, I could see Sandy restraining her emotions. Biting her lip and holding back tears, she waited until everyone else in her group had shared their reflections before she finally disclosed hers.

Her early memory came from a time when she was five or six years old, a time, she recalled, when her family lived next to a group home for the developmentally disabled. When her family moved there they immediately put up a high chain-link fence between their property and the group home. During the two years she lived in the house, she remembered that any time she went outside to play, her mother vigilantly watched her and her siblings. If they got close to the chain-link fence she would yell with horror in her voice, "Get away from that fence! Those people are dirty and they'll hurt you!" Sandy had uncovered the source of her guilt-ridden thoughts. In all these years working with the developmentally disabled, she hadn't consciously recalled that memory. Yet, unconsciously, it was still there and affecting her thoughts on a regular basis.

Sandy had, for the first time, clearly seen one of her automatic filters.

As we know, our filters are formed by our past experiences. Like Sandy, we don't typically recall the past experience itself, just the judgment or determination that was made during that past experience. And in simpler instances, especially those not involving other people, the filter is beneficial. You may or may not remember the actual experience of touching a hot flame for the first time, but you do know that it's not a good thing to do; you know that it will hurt you, and so you avoid it.

Our brains are almost frighteningly efficient. They need to move with unbelievable speed through a lifetime of stored information to construct immediate decisions about how we should react from moment to moment. This efficiency manifests in the creation of a judgmental shorthand—you guessed it— automatic filters. We believe them to be true even if many times we're presented with contradictory information.

Unbroken Filters

Recently I had an experience where I was made vividly aware of one of my own automatic filters. I had just walked out of a movie theater into the frigid air when I was stopped cold. It wasn't the temperature, though at minus ten degrees that day it would have been the most obvious explanation. It was something even more powerful. It was one of my filters. There it was, right in front of me. I froze for a couple of seconds, amazed at how quickly and how strongly this filter had colored my perception of my then current reality.

I had taken my daughters to see the movie *Unbroken*, the story of Louis Zamperini—the Olympic runner who was held as a prisoner of war in Japanese camps during WWII. It was a gripping and emotional movie about the resilience of Zamperini in the face of all that evil and violence. We watched nearly two hours of nonstop brutality—both mental and physical torture with one beating after another perpetrated by Japanese soldiers, and one Japanese officer in particular.

As we walked out into the lobby at the end of the movie, I told my girls I would run to get the car so they wouldn't have to go out in the cold. It was on my walk to the car a couple of blocks away that my automatic filters caused a SEEing problem. Hunched over, braced against the cold, I turned a corner and was startled by two men walking toward me. It was a bright sunny afternoon in a busy area—no reason for me to feel afraid of two men walking down the street. Yet I actually felt a split-second of terror.

It wasn't because they were men. It was because they were Asian.

My brain had just been bombarded with image after image of a Japanese man as a malicious torturer. While I was passively being entertained, watching a movie, my unconscious was busy gathering those images and prescribing a new filter for me to see the world through. That prescription equated Japanese men with evil and fear. It created new perceptions and new judgment, and it did all of this *unconsciously*. I wasn't sitting in the movie theater consciously thinking that now I should see all Japanese men differently. My unconscious mind made those decisions for me and manifested them as automatic filters, dropped in place and ready to go as I walked out of the theater.

The decision had already been made about how I should perceive and respond to these two men. It didn't matter that they might have good intentions toward me. It didn't matter that I'm a diversity consultant, live this stuff every day, and so should know better. It didn't matter that I grew up with a stream of Japanese students in my home as exchange students. It didn't matter that the two men weren't even Japanese—I believe they were actually Hmong. Filters involving people are rarely accurate, rarely anticipated, and almost always in control.

> Filters involving people are rarely accurate, rarely anticipated, and almost always in control.

After the initial jolt of filtered perception, I found myself in the moment marveling at the power of automatic filters. Like the neuroscientist Jill Bolte Taylor[5], who marveled at the opportunity to witness her own brain as she was having a stroke, I found myself observing my brain in action through the consciously created filter of my work. I wasn't in control of the *initial* thoughts and feelings that my unconscious automatic filters sent to my conscious brain. But after that, I *purposefully* Filter Shifted. I recognized that the thoughts and feelings had come from filters most immediately created by the movie, and reinforced by countless other filters

---

5   Jill Bolte Taylor, Ph.D., *My Stroke of Insight: A Brain Scientist's Personal Journey* (Penguin, 2008); TED talk: Jill Bolte Taylor, Ph.D., *My Stroke of Insight* (March 2008).

being shuffled into place by my unconscious. These filters were all connected *only to images and events in my past* and fell into place to show me what *felt real* but was in fact completely (in this case especially) illusory.

Applying Filter Shift

My first Filter Shift consisted of acknowledging that these men were obviously not even Japanese. Asian, yes, but not Japanese. Our filters don't always focus down to levels of specificity or granularity when attaching a value to a person or thing. Again, their efficiency comes from the unconscious using them to lump together things that it categorizes as similar. After your first experience with touching a flame your filters are created, and you may well equate pain with *all* things hot, not just a flame. In my case, the label of torturer and source of fear at that first moment extended to all Asian men.

Our automatic filters effectively *filter out* complexity.

My next Filter Shift enabled me to clearly identify that I wasn't in danger. The two men were actually laughing, giving off no signals that they even noticed me, much less wanted to harm me. But of greater interest to me was the realization that even after I assessed there was no danger, I *still* had negative feelings toward these men for no reason that actually tied to the present conscious moment. All the negative feelings came from the prescriptions of my unconscious, and all of those were tied to past moments. That meant that my unconscious was pulling from my past to determine how to experience the present. Yet I had had years of positive experiences as a child with Japanese exchange students living in my house. Shouldn't those years of positive experience outweigh these last couple of hours of negative experience?

Under the Influence

I knew as I was processing all of this that unfortunately that isn't the case. Our unconscious is far less concerned with the past than the immediate present. Therefore, the filters being used don't only go back into the recesses of our memories. Instead, the filter lenses are layered, accessing the most recent experience, naturally the most intense, first, with older experiences coloring the final "reallusion" to a greater or lesser degree depending on their distance from the present. We have evidence of this in examples of negative bias being reduced after a recent dose of positive images.

Even more confounding, as I saw those two men, was that not only did my unconscious only access my most *recent* experience, but that "experience" wasn't even mine! I'm not the one that was a brutalized prisoner in a Japanese war camp. I only experienced the brutality second-hand. However, our unconscious *doesn't distinguish between the two*. It just takes in the information, processes it, and holds onto it to help it prescribe decisions down the road. It doesn't matter if we received that information from a newscast, from water cooler gossip, from

> A major consequence of our unconscious acceptance of the judgment provided by our automatic filters, whatever their source, is that so many of us end up with very strong opinions about other groups, even individuals, with whom we've actually had very little, if any, personal contact.

an image we saw, or from an experience we actually had. All that information is *equally likely* to influence us at some time in the future. A major consequence of our unconscious acceptance of the judgment provided by our automatic filters, whatever their source, is that so many of us end up with very strong opinions about other groups, even individuals, with whom we've actually had very little, if any, personal contact.

And how would we ever get to know another person anyway? With all these automatic filters blurring our vision, how can we ever trust what we think we see?

Contradicting Filters

Not only may our filters be inaccurate, they may also be the exact opposite of others' filters. For example:

- The filters of an extrovert tell them that talking through their ideas to figure out next steps is normal, good, and professional. The filters of the introvert tell them that normal, good, and professional behavior would actually be to reflect and contemplate quietly on their own.

- The direct communicator will talk face-to-face with the person they are in conflict with and elucidate in detail their concerns, because their filters tell them that is the way they show respect for the other individual. The indirect communicator will show respect by using inferences, stories, metaphors, and may even use a third party to relay the information, because their filters tell them that is the respectful way to deal with conflict.

- The filters of different generations (boomers, Generation X, millennials, etc.) each describe the value of work differently.
- The filters of a relationship-centered individual pass judgment on the task-oriented individual and label them as rude. Conversely, the filters of a task-oriented individual see the behavior of a relationship-oriented individual as inefficient, wasting time, and off task.

When we believe our filters to be true, it's easy to see how misunderstandings arise even with the best of intentions. We need to take our skill building one step further—to teach ourselves to see the *Frames* to which our Filters are attached in the first place.

• • • Key Points • • •

- Our filters are:
  - the stored information in our brain that our unconscious uses to evaluate situations and make decisions
  - formed and operate in our unconscious, which we don't access, so typically are automatic
  - created by our past experiences and become the lenses through which we view our current experiences
  - typically much more powerful than we realize
  - sometimes wrong
  - typically cloud complexity
  - at times the exact opposite of others' filters.

Chapter Five

Frames—What We Typically Pay Attention To

H er senses were heightened, her mouth dry, and the flutter of anticipation in her stomach wouldn't go away. These were her very first parent-teacher conferences. Becky had been a student teacher for two months now. While the first day of teaching with her students had been hard, she didn't anticipate that this evening could be any more difficult.

She had set up a special spot in her third-grade classroom where she planned to sit with the parents to discuss their children's progress. Because this was a poor inner-city school, they didn't have any extra adult-sized chairs. Around the group reading table she had arranged a couple of folding chairs borrowed from her parents, who lived in a small farming community a couple of hours away.

Ever since she could remember, Becky had wanted to be a teacher. In some ways, this just felt like a continuation of the many times she played teacher growing up. Yet now she knew the stakes were high. These were real kids, real parents, and real challenges.

The evening started well with, as Becky described them, two quiet, respectful Mexican families that were intentionally scheduled back-to-back because they needed the school translator to interpret. She could feel the regard they held for her as a teacher even though she was obviously much younger than they. It was the third conference that sent the evening down a very different path—her first of many African American families of the night, and Becky noticed that she felt nervous. She wondered why.

"Yes, I'm white," Becky thought, "but I don't know why I should be nervous. They're just like me. We all want what's best for these kids."

In Over Our Heads

The conference began without incident as LaKeisha's mother, Kim, started the conversation talking about the school's overall test scores and how unfortunate it was that they were a little lower this year. It was when Becky directed the conversation to LaKeisha and her personal test scores and grades that Becky felt like she lost control of the conference.

As Becky later described it, "Kim was out of control. As soon as we started talking about the D her daughter was getting in math she started yelling at me, asking what I was going to do about that D and that I had to tell her what *she* was supposed to do about that D. She even slammed her hand on the table as she practically shouted that no daughter of hers was going to get a D." Becky was still shaken by the experience two weeks later as she recounted it.

"I told her she had to calm down so we could talk about it, and she actually said, 'I am calm!'"

As Becky relayed her own thoughts during the interaction, she described both confusion and fear. She didn't understand the mother's response and actually felt frightened about what the mother might do to her.

Also running through her mind was the class she had just taken the semester before about managing classroom behavior. She had learned how important it was not to allow disruptive, unproductive behavior and to maintain control in the classroom. Sure, this was a parent not a student, but it was still her classroom and she shouldn't tolerate behavior that was disrespectful.

So Becky essentially did what she would have done with one of her third graders. She gave Kim a time-out.

Time-out Fallout

"Of course I didn't call it a time-out, but that's what I was thinking. I just told her that I wanted her to take a break out in the hall while I did my next conference and that when she calmed down we could talk about LaKeisha's D." Becky had no idea how much that approach would damage her relationship with Kim and LaKeisha. Feeling offended, Kim told Becky she was just a clueless little white girl from the farm that was in way over her head. She threatened to talk to the principal and, without even waiting for a response, turned and walked out the door.

Becky was devastated about the conference. As she sat through our training and learned about the concept of frames, she became both embarrassed and relieved. She realized that the actual root of the problem with that conference wasn't an issue of respect, but a difference in one specific *frame*—our cultural styles of communication.[6]

In that training we described two distinct styles: emotionally expressive and emotionally restrained. Both styles, while exhibiting almost completely opposite behavior, have the same underlying value of respect and are taught by different cultural groups as the right way to communicate.

As you can imagine, Becky's style was the opposite of Kim's. As an emotionally restrained communicator, Becky may feel intense emotion but wouldn't express that outwardly.

She remembered her mother always saying that emotions got in the way of solving problems. So when Becky was incredibly angry and approaching conflict, her tone of voice wasn't much different from when she was excited and happy. Her physical gestures, if any, were very small and close to her body. Kim, on the other hand, was very likely emotionally expressive. With this style, emotions are expressed outwardly with large vocalizations, distinct change of tone, and large, expressive gestures.

Expressing emotion from the perspective of this style is a way to show passion for an issue. Kim's expression of her passion for

6   M.R. Hammer (2005). The intercultural conflict style inventory: A conceptual framework and measure of intercultural conflict resolution approaches. *International Journal of Intercultural Relations*, volume 29, pages 675-695.

her daughter's grades was likely a signal to Becky that the issue was incredibly important to her and she wanted to resolve it.

Becky now realized that when she told Kim to calm down, she was essentially telling her not to care about her daughter's education. Sending her out of the room because she was expressing passion about her daughter's grades was disrespectful, audacious and, as Kim described it in the moment, clueless. Becky now understood why both Kim and LaKeisha had been so cold and distant with her since the conference.

Both mother and teacher were passionate about LaKeisha's education and wanted to figure out how to help the student succeed. Yet, because they were focused on and couldn't get beyond their differing frames, they weren't able to come together to work toward their common goal.

A Frame for All Seasons

Frames attract our attention. They are the things that are visible and that we can easily see, such as our physical characteristics—our race, color, gender, size, beauty. They are also fundamental behaviors and actions that trigger automatic filters to drop into place, priming us with illusions of certainty.

Frames attract our attention. They are the things that are visible and that we can easily see, such as our physical characteristics—our race, color, gender, size, beauty. They are also fundamental behaviors and actions that trigger automatic filters to drop into place.

In this case, race was the first frame that Becky focused on and was worried about. She related the discomfort she had with the frame of race to the frame of the different communication styles. She was already a bit uncomfortable; then, faced with the different communication style, she was actually afraid.

Our focus on frames can get in the way as we try to be effective because we rarely view a frame objectively. With clarity obscured by automatic filters, we often misidentify the intent behind observed behavior as well as observed appearance. Frames are what we *actually* see. Our automatic filters are how we interpret and place judgment on that. Or, in other words, what we *think* we see.

A Part of and Apart From

There is a concept in cognitive psychology that helps us understand frames a bit better. We know that all of our brains do the same thing. Regardless of where we come from, our race, ethnicity, or how we were raised, we all do the same thing as we approach others. We create "in-groups" and "out-groups."

As we approach others, our brains furiously begin to categorize them and our relation to them as either *a part of* or *apart from*. When we walk into a room of people we instantly analyze and determine where we fit and where we don't fit. Even in a family reunion where essentially we are a part of the whole group, we still categorize those we are a little more a part of and those we are a little more apart from.

When it's a roomful of strangers, this categorization is based solely on frames, the things we more readily pay attention to both consciously and unconsciously because we can immediately see them.

Our brains are hardwired to perform this analysis. For our Neanderthal predecessors it was a necessary function to determine threat. While most modern humans don't experience a constant threat of death, our brains still hold on to this function and lead us to constantly unconsciously categorize each other.

This determining function is designed to help us decide when we should be acting differently, maybe holding our guard up and paying more attention, as well as when we can let our guard down and relax.

Unfortunately, the more complex the social situation, the more likely our brains will be wrong. That can leave us paying attention to things that actually aren't impacting the current situation, or ignoring other more important things that are making a difference.

The in-group/out-group determination that our unconscious mind makes starts with frames—that person looks *like* me, they go to my *same* church, my *same* gym, they share the *same* hobby . . . things we can easily see. However, as we saw last chapter, the final arbiter of acceptance or rejection is the perception created by our filters. It becomes almost impossible to see the ways in which those who seem *like* us might in fact be different, and the ways in which those who seem *different* might actually be similar.

The Jiving Hand

Tonya could relate to this. She didn't know exactly why it bothered her so much because she knew people had good intentions, so she almost felt guilty about how much it did bother her.

As a young African American in a mostly white organization, all too often her white coworkers would greet her differently than they would great each other, with an expressive "Hey giiiiiirl!" in a feeble attempt to relate to her with a verbal jive. One coworker even approached her with a jumbled attempt at a hand-jive handshake. Each of them, while well-intentioned, focused on a frame and approached Tonya with filters in place, not realizing they were actually offending her.

Organizations do this too. We can hear it in how they approach us with their requests. "We have a group of executives that will be going to Japan next month. Can you give them training on the top twenty things they should know about Japan and the top twenty behaviors they need to be aware of? We know that bowing is important, but what else should they know about?" The underlying belief is that these executives just need to change a few behaviors—frames—and then they can get on with the business at hand and be successful in the interaction.

> The reality is that those frames elicit an automatically filtered response, and without an understanding of the filters, they can't clearly see the frames.

The reality is that those frames elicit an automatically filtered response, and without an understanding of the filters, they can't clearly see the frames.

As with many other skills, we need to have a cognitive understanding before we can successfully exhibit a different behavior. In essence, teaching them how to bow would be just like teaching Tonya's coworkers how to hand-jive. Their behavior, like that of Tonya's colleagues, would seem inauthentic and superficial.

That's because it wouldn't be rooted in a clear view of the frame itself.

Bowing in Japan is an expression of the filter of respect. The US executives traveling there need to understand that filter, coupled with the filter of the importance of hierarchy in Japan. If not, they will do as I am told one executive did when traveling to Japan. Paying attention only to the frame, unaware of his own occluding filters, he lost a significant business deal with his Japanese clients because they saw him bow just as deeply to the hotel maid as he had bowed to them, his potential clients—a significant sign of disrespect.

It's not just as we attempt to look across the gap to other individuals that this comes into play. At times we experience a dissonance when we're confused about our *own* frames. I hear this often during individual coaching sessions. From the white American that said she just didn't see herself fitting in that box with other white Americans, to the mixed-race college student who says he didn't see himself as either Asian like his mom or white like his dad. These identity crises exist because they're trying to define themselves by their *frames* while still seeing through their own *filters*—trying to define *what's actually there* by *what their filters tell them is there.*

Full Spectrum SEEing

The graphic of our filters and frames can help us understand how the two relate to one another. We are typically aware of our frames and unaware of our filters (see fig. 5.1). Yet misunderstanding and conflict are due to a difference in filters, not frames.

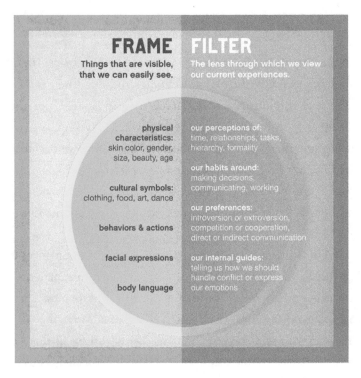

Figure 5.1. Our frames are primarily in our awareness while our filters are primarily out of our awareness.

Think of it this way: Jose and Joe are coworkers. Jose, a brown-skinned Latino, grew up in the Southwest eating rice and beans and still considers them a comfort food today. Joe, on the other hand, is a white, fourth-generation American who grew up in the Midwest on mashed potatoes and gravy and still considers those comfort foods. All of those differences are easy-to-see *frames*.

However, they each also have different *filters* that aren't so easy to see. Jose's filters focus on relationships. It's important for him to connect with his colleagues as people, and he believes he can only get his work done well when he has strong connections to his coworkers. Joe's filters, on the other hand, focus on tasks. He just wants to get through his task list as soon as he can regardless of—and sometimes, he would say, in spite of—his coworkers.

Put Joe and Jose together on a team and will it be the easy-to-see frames of rice versus potatoes that get in the way? No, it will be their filters.

• • • Key Points • • •

- Our frames are:
    - what we typically use to categorize others as "a part of" or "apart from"
    - the things we can easily see such as our race, color, gender, size, age
    - also the outward, visible behaviors and actions
    - what we typically pay attention to and focus on to make judgments about ourselves and others
    - what can distract us from what is making more of a difference and what is really in control, our filters
    - what we oftentimes focus on when trying to adapt to others, when it is actually our filters that we need to be aware of in order to be more effective
    - what we are typically aware of versus our filters, of which we are typically unaware. Yet misunderstanding and conflict are often due to a difference in filters, not frames.

Chapter Six

It's Developmental

t was an afternoon of back-to-back coaching calls. I had just talked to five supervisors all from the same department. The calls were for the purpose of reviewing their individual IDI® assessment results, so we were discussing their levels of cultural competence.[7] It struck me that while they worked in the same department, these five individuals described a very different workplace.

"I'm really not even around people that are different from me."

---

7   M.R. Hammer (2012). The Intercultural Development Inventory: A new frontier in assessment and development of intercultural competence. In M. Vande Berg, R.M. Paige, & K.H. Lou (Eds.), *Student Learning Abroad* (Ch. 5, pp. 115-136). Sterling, VA: Stylus Publishing.

"I love the fact that we have so much more diversity in the department now. It makes things so much more interesting, and I love hearing how other people see things differently."

"We have a lot of problems because of all of those people that work here now. Some of them you can't even understand, and others don't really want to work."

"We all get along really well. We're like a family. We have a lot of differences, but we're strong and we don't focus on our differences because that just brings conflict."

"Frankly, I get really frustrated. We have so much diversity around us that we don't do anything to fully utilize."

How could five people have five very different descriptions of the same department in the same organization?

This sounds like the proverbial example of five blindfolded individuals describing the different part of the elephant that they're personally touching, and believing it to be the whole animal; each individual has a different perspective based on where they are standing.

While it's certainly true, as we've seen in the previous chapters, that we all do indeed have different perspectives, in this case that's not the reason for the variety of responses. In this case, the responses are reflective of five distinct *stages of development.*

The field of cultural competence has identified those stages through a number of similar developmental frameworks: the Developmental Model of Intercultural Sensitivity by Milton

Bennett;[8] the Cultural Competence Continuum by Terry Cross;[9] and the Intercultural Development Continuum by Mitchell Hammer.[10] Each of these three models uses various names for the stages. I principally use and refer to Hammer's model in my work, and here, instead of names for the stages, I am simply using the labels of 1-5 (see fig. 6.1).

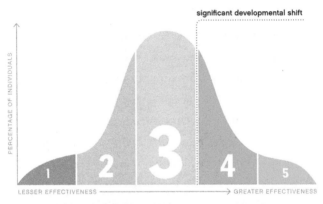

Figure 6.1. We develop from stages of lesser effectiveness to greater effectiveness as we interact across difference. Few of us have reached the stages of higher effectiveness and the majority of us are in the

8   Milton J. Bennett (1993). Towards Ethnorelativism: A Developmental Model of Intercultural Sensitivity. In Paige, R.M. (Ed). *Education for the Intercultural Experience* (2nd ed.) Yarmouth, ME: Intercultural Press.

9   Cross T., Bazron, B., Dennis, K., & Isaacs, M. (1989). *Towards a Culturally Competent System of Care*, Volume I. Washington, DC: Georgetown University Child Development Center, CASSP Technical Assistance Center.

10 Hammer, M. (2012). The Intercultural Development Inventory: A new frontier in assessment and development of intercultural competence. In M. Vande Berg, R.M. Paige, & K.H. Lou (Eds.), *Student Learning Abroad* (Ch. 5, pp. 115-136). Sterling, VA: Stylus Publishing.

middle stage—the last of the ineffective stages. Moving into the last and most effective stages requires a significant developmental shift.

What do all of these models teach us? Among other things, that our experience of difference is *developmental*.

In the case of these supervisors, their experiences in the organization were a reflection of those five different stages of development and therefore different stages of effectiveness as they interacted across difference.

When we get down to it, that's what these stages reveal: effectiveness. Only in the last stage are we able to be our most effective. Learning how to Filter Shift helps us more efficiently reduce our bias and get to that higher level of effectiveness.

> **Only in the last stage are we able to be our most effective. Learning how to Filter Shift helps us more efficiently reduce our bias and get to that higher level of effectiveness.**

Unfortunately, very few of us—2.5 percent to be exact—are in this last stage of development. This statistic comes from the IDI, an assessment developed by Hammer used to measure where we're at on this model. In fact, thanks to the IDI® we can see that the percentages of individuals in the 5 stages follows a normative distribution, or a bell curve, with a smaller number of individuals, 2.5 percent, in the first and last stages, 13.5 percent in stages 2 and 4, and the majority, 68 percent, in the middle or third stage.

Stage 1

Her intent was to be kind, caring, and friendly; her impact was anything but. Evelyn, the hospital volunteer assigned to assist families of surgery patients, wanted to connect with each of the families and provide them comfort. Often referred to as the resident "grandma," Evelyn was a well-known fixture in the hospital. Her endless enthusiasm and constant energy defied her octogenarian age. It was over twenty years ago that she started volunteering as a patient liaison, wanting to still be active after her retirement from her forty-year career as a secretary. She seemed to know everyone who worked at the hospital by first name and was known for telling each one of them that she loved them—and meaning it.

When the volunteer coordinator pulled her aside to inform her they had received a complaint from the Jones family, who had been deeply offended by her, she was stunned.

As she sat in front of the volunteer coordinator in the cramped side office, she remembered the Jones family and recalled warm feelings for them.

The patient was a twenty-year-old black man having a not-so-routine surgery, which left his family justifiably concerned and anxious. His fifty-year-old father, John, the stately, respected leader of the family, assumed the responsibility of liaison with hospital staff to ensure that if there was any bad news, he could be the one to pass it on to the rest of his family.

Evelyn couldn't think of anything she had said or done that would have been offensive to them. She was certainly never rude to them. Even when the coordinator asked her if she remembered calling fifty-year-old John "boy," Evelyn still didn't make the connection.

It had to be made for her.

She had to be told that John, as a fifty-year-old black man, was offended when she continued to refer to him as "boy." "I was just trying to be nice. If someone were to call me girl, I would appreciate that. It would make me feel young! I just wanted him to know he was young in my eyes." When asked if she likewise addressed fifty-year-old white men as boys, she said she couldn't recall, but that it shouldn't matter.

The coordinator went on to explain that historically the term "boy" has been used to denigrate and emasculate black men. Evelyn felt both horrified to think that John would have taken her language in the same vein and also indignant that she only meant to be kind and caring. She felt positive that those intentions should somehow outweigh the negative impact of her words.

In this situation, Evelyn was operating in the first stage of development where we are oblivious to differences, even those that are easy to see. She wasn't even aware of a significant difference in the frame that was at play. When we operate in this stage we tend to avoid differences, or are just not interested in interacting across those differences. In this stage, we don't know *what* we don't know—we also *don't know* that we don't know it.

To shift out of this stage, as Bennett first identified, we need to start seeing the surface-level differences; i.e., the easy-to-see frames that are around us. For individuals, that can mean going to the international festival to watch the Chinese dragon dancers, or stopping to get groceries at the Mexican market instead of the mainstream supermarket.

As we start to see the surface-level differences in our frames, we move out of this stage and into the second, where we are compelled to make right/wrong and good/bad judgments about them.

Stage 2

It was a perfect setting for a barbecue: warm sun, no bugs, and good company. Yet in short time, the conversation was sizzling even more than the grill.

Years ago, not long after our first daughter was born, my husband Miguel and I were invited to a Sunday afternoon picnic at the home of Barb and Steve, another young couple we were anxious to become better acquainted with. Like us, they were new parents with young, demanding kids and young, demanding careers. I think we all hoped that Sunday barbecue would bring a much needed respite to our daily chaos.

As the kids played and the meat grilled, we began a conversation that quickly turned to our new roles as parents.

Miguel and I had recently been talking quite a bit with each other about the values and traditions we wanted for our own family. As a bicultural couple—Miguel from the Dominican Republic and me from the United States—we felt like we had a rich opportunity to consciously create the culture of our family, choosing specific parts from each of our own respective cultures. Excited about this vision for our family, Miguel and I were eager to talk about it, particularly with another couple in the same stage of parenting as us.

Both Barb and Steve were born and raised in the United States and had never traveled outside of the country. As we were explaining our vision for our family, we found ourselves describing the aspects that came from the Dominican culture, since those were the aspects with which they likely wouldn't be familiar.

We talked about Dominicans' heightened respect for elders, their focus on the group more than the individual, and their more emotionally expressive communication style. With each description we became more and more animated, eager to talk about the values that we could envision in our new family.

As we moved through these descriptions, I noticed Steve start to anxiously tap the table with a beer bottle cap that he had been playing with. One eyebrow raised in a growing look of disapproval as he pursed his lips trying to hold back his comments. Increasing in intensity, his bottle-cap taps finally stopped when he burst out, "What is your problem with Americans anyway? Why do you think America is so bad?"

Miguel and I were confused. We actually hadn't even mentioned America—or the US, as we would have called it—much less any negative feelings or judgments about it. Yet, from the mindset of the second stage of development, when you're saying something good about one group, it means you're implicitly saying something bad about the other.

This second stage of development is very polarizing. While we weren't actually saying anything about American culture, from this us/them mindset, to say something positive about Dominicans—the "them"—means we were saying something negative about Americans—the "us."

Think of it as a balance scale where we put ourselves and our group—people with similar frames—on the one side, and groups that are different from us on the other side. That's the us/them dynamic. Because there is also a good/bad dynamic, one side of the scale is up and the group on that side is seen more positively, while the other side is down and that group is seen more negatively. Unlike the other stages, Stage 2 manifests in two ways, depending on which group we identify with more positively.

My Group Is Good; Others Are Bad

In the most extreme cases this is where we have the hate groups like the skinheads, the Nazis, or the Ku Klux Klan. Fortunately, in the workplace we don't often see these extreme examples, but you might hear statements from this stage such as, "Why do we have to translate our materials? They're in America; they should speak American."

Our automatic filters are dropping into place, making it hard to SEE the actual situation or individual clearly. We make instant, *subjective* judgments of what's right or wrong. This happens so regularly and so quickly, we accept these judgments as *objectively* true and then attach them globally to specific frames. We look at a tree, and our filters show us a forest of judgments like:

- "You can't trust people who don't speak up in a meeting. The ones that just sit there thinking? Nope, you just can't trust them."

- "How can you expect her to have phone conversation skills? She's too young. She only knows how to text. Of course she's going to get low customer service scores on the phone."

- "How many more of them do you want to hire? Don't you think we have enough already?"

- "I think he's probably too old to do this job. He won't understand technology."

While we might easily see how this manifestation of Stage 2 can be offensive, the same isn't always true for the second manifestation—when we identify *other* groups more positively, seeing them as better than our group.

My Group Is Bad; Others Are Good

Mary could easily see how this alternate manifestation of Stage 2 showed up for her. As a female executive in a male-dominated industry, and in the latter stage of her long career, she had numerous experiences of being the only woman in the room.

"The only way I could survive early on was to fit in and become one of the guys."

As a result, Mary hardened her approach to be more masculine and learned how to interrupt others to get her point added to the mix, and even though her emotions were present, she tried to ignore them and not allow them to enter into decision making—just as she saw her male counterparts do. She even remembered in the early days that she actually wore men's suits and ties to the office.

"In the workplace I've always distanced myself from anything that would highlight my gender."

That's why Mary had a bad reputation with younger women leaders. She was harder on them and often rejected their requests for her to mentor them. When they asked her to be a part of the women in leadership employee group, her response was a resounding "NO."

"I don't want to be seen as a *woman* leader; I just want to be seen as a leader, and don't they realize they just need to pull themselves up by their bootstraps?"

Through my coaching with Mary, she was able to begin seeing that while that strategy may have helped her years ago, it was now keeping her from being her most effective.

The same is very true for another common manifestation of reversal, *white guilt*. I often hear well-intentioned whites—who have become aware of the many benefits they receive in our society because of the color of their skin—speak poorly of their own race. While the awareness of the power and privilege is commendable, holding on to the categorical and judgmental view of one group over another keeps us in Stage 2.

That, in turn, keeps us from being our most effective because in this stage we're not able to see beyond our frames. Therefore, our experience of ourselves and others is very shallow, lacking the rich complexity we see in later stages. It is also very narrow, categorizing people and groups monolithically.

Our filters cause us to attach generalized judgments to particular frames. Yet since our frames don't determine how well we perform or what we value, when we only rely on our filters, unconscious ones at that, we are making a direct connection that may very well *not exist*.

To shift from this stage, we need to balance the scale and focus on commonalities.

Early in my career I worked in a rural community that was experiencing this stage as they faced an influx of immigrants. Because of conflicts, mistrust, and fear between the long-established community and the new immigrant communities, as well as within each of the immigrant communities themselves, we held a meeting bringing together each of the community groups' leaders.

The division was palpable in the room until we processed our "20/20" activity. It asked them what kind of a community they wanted twenty years from now. After each group discussed at their tables and reported back to the larger group, they realized that they all wanted essentially the same things—good education for their kids, a safe community, and good jobs for their families. They realized they all had something in common. With that realization, they could begin to see each other with less *judgment* and more *understanding*.

This focus on commonalities brings us firmly into the third and most prevalent stage, where we shy away from pointing out differences.

Stage 3

"A focus on differences divides. A focus on similarity unites." That's the mindset of this third stage where most of us exist—in fact, 68 percent of us according to the IDI®. Here we move beyond seeing differences as a threat, though we still aren't able to be our most effective. That's because we can't see the complexity that's involved in our interactions. We get stuck here. That's both because we promote this stage to each other, as I described in chapter three, and

> We get stuck here. That's both because we promote this stage to each other, as I described in chapter three, and because developmentally it's a challenge to move out of this stage.

because developmentally it's a challenge to move out of this stage (see fig. 6.1). I'll explain that significant developmental shift more in the next chapter. Knowing how to Filter Shift can alleviate these challenges and serve as our "Teflon" to ensure we don't get stuck here. It helps us to finally move to the effective stages, the last two stages.

Stage 4

"It's like the Wizard of Oz!" This is how Cheryl described her change in mindset. "You know the scene where it magically shifts from the grainy black-and-white images to the full high-definition color? That's what this has been like for me."

I had just delivered Cheryl's encouraging IDI® assessment results. After a nine-month process working with Cheryl and her colleagues—a leadership team in a Denver-based healthcare organization—Cheryl had significantly advanced her competence from the left side of the continuum to the far right side. To her, that difference was like being able to see in full color for the first time. She described how she hadn't even realized what she had been blind to. Previously she had no idea so much was going on around her. Becoming aware of her own biases and learning to see the distortions caused by her automatic filters, she suddenly realized the rich complexity of differences that had been there all along. "It's not that they weren't there before; it's just that I couldn't see them. When I couldn't see them, I was missing out."

This fourth stage acknowledges different filters without judging them. Here there are two significant ways we approach differences more effectively. First, we are able to see beyond the surface level and experience greater complexity. Second, we see that complexity without judgment.

Greater Complexity

As if entering the Land of Oz, complexity begins to come alive in the fourth stage, the first of the effective stages. For the first time we clearly see the complex web of filters—both our own and others'—and how they influence every interaction.

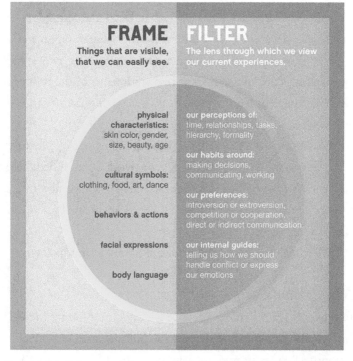

Figure 6.2. Filters and frames. As we develop our effectiveness from left to right on the Development Continuum, we become more able to see the filters that are typically out of our awareness.

We start to see that it is our filters, not our frames, which determine how we make decisions, how we communicate, how we decide what is good, right, and professional. We therefore understand that since others have different filters, their determination of good, right, and professional might also be different in any given situation.

Remember this image of our frames, which are primarily in our awareness, together with our filters, which are primarily out of our awareness (see fig. 6.2)? When we operate in the first three stages of the continuum—what I call the left side—the easy-to-see differences of our frames are what tend to get in the way. For some of us, particularly in the first two stages, that's because our discomfort with or judgment of the frames of others distracts us from what is really impacting the situation—the filters of us both.

For others—the majority of us in the third stage—what gets in the way is our well-intentioned, yet naïve and misguided, belief that comfort with different frames equals competence in our interactions across those differences. Remember False Prescription #6: Comfort doesn't equal competence.

We realize the truth of this for the first time in this stage.

Complexity Is Richness

Take a look again at the graphic of the filters and frames (fig 6.1). The graphic as a whole represents the full spectrum of difference. Yet only when we begin operating in the fourth stage do we have access to the richness of that full spectrum.

When we're operating on the left side of the first three stages of the spectrum (see fig. 6.2), we only have access to the top sphere, which represents our frames. We have access to just the differences of race, gender, behaviors, language, etc.

Until we reach the fourth stage, we're missing out because only beginning in this stage are we able to also see the bottom sphere of our filters. That's why the ability to Filter Shift is so important. Only with that ability are we able to tap into that great richness.

SEEing Clearly

Joe and Jose with their differences in frame—rice and potatoes—versus their differences in filters—task and relationship—help us see why this stage is so important to our effectiveness. An understanding of the filters involved on *both sides* brings greater clarity to what's actually impacting us and others.

One analogy of that clarity and detail is a portrait. A portrait painted by someone operating on the left side of the development spectrum of a person they're interacting with would be made up of just a few broad brushstrokes, because they only have a few points of detail to describe the other person. A portrait painted by someone operating on the right side of the spectrum would be a pointillism painting made up of a million different points of detail representing the complexity they are able to see in that person.

Seeing the Tree While Still Appreciating the Forest

Back to Cheryl. As she and I talked about her newly acquired competence, she said what surprised her most was that she uses it all the time with "people that before I would have said are just like me. They look like me, live in my same small community, and our kids play on the same soccer team. Now I can see that they are actually very different from me."

When we only pay attention to frames, as Cheryl had in the past, and we don't see differences at that level, we assume similarity, which causes us to miss out on the complexity of differences in our filters.

In the fourth stage, operating on the right side of the spectrum, we learn that a homogenous group *by appearance* doesn't equate with a group that is *actually* the same.

This Is This, That Is That

There is another significant way we approach differences more effectively. In Stage 4 we are able to see our filters without placing value or judgment on them. We know they are just different—not good or bad—just different.

Sally is my reminder of this ability. One of my fellow Peace Corps volunteers, she frequently talked about Dominicans and the Dominican culture from a fourth-stage perspective.

One warm afternoon a group of us sat rocking in our *mesadoras* on the porch of the Peace Corps office, pleasantly reconnecting with our fellow volunteer friends. Then the conversation turned negative, thanks to Joe, who seemed to be continually complaining about Dominicans and the Dominican Republic in general. In this particular conversation, his grievances happened to be about a lack of privacy he had been experiencing in his *campo* and an overall lack of individualism.

With a general sense of disdain, he said, "Have you ever noticed that Dominicans are never alone? Think about it. No one lives alone; they are always together in groups, and every time I walk in my door, twenty kids follow at my heels and try to walk in with me! It drives me crazy!"

As Sally joined us a few minutes later and heard the gist of the conversation, her response came purely from the fourth stage. She simply acknowledged the complexity of the difference without judgment. "That whole group thing? I know, that's just so Dominican, isn't it?"

Because we are able to see the greater complexities that are influencing the situations we are in, we can be much more effective in this stage. In fact, this is the first of the effective stages not only because we can see that complexity, but also because we can better match our intent with the impact *and* more clearly see the intent of others.

The goal is to see our own filters in a nonjudgmental way. They are no longer the absolute (or obvious, commonsensical, good, right, and professional way); they are just one option. Once we can see our own filters in this way, we are able to see the filters of others without judging them as good or bad. We see how their filters determine their frames. Seeing differences in this way, we are more open to them and actually seek them out.

To move beyond this fourth stage to the fifth and final stage, we need to practice approaching situations differently.

Stage 5

Only in the final stage are we able to see from others'

> Only in the final stage are we able to see from others' perspectives. This means we are able to actually SEE others' filters and use those different criteria to understand and make sense of (interpret and evaluate) the situation at hand.

perspectives. This means we are able to actually SEE others' filters and use those different criteria to understand and make sense of (interpret and evaluate) the situation at hand. We're essentially able to *think like others are thinking*, which in turn allows us the opportunity to see our own filters from the perspective of another.

Because the shift in filters can naturally produce a shift in our behavior, we are also frame shifting. We start to act differently with different people, in different groups, or different situations. We adapt our behavior to be more effective and can even serve as a bridge between groups.

This isn't *assimilation*. We aren't relinquishing our own filters or frames but rather utilizing other filters and frames, in a given situation, to be more effective.

Just as a math student progresses through levels of math to become proficient, so too do we progress through these developmental stages to become more effective. The math student needs to learn basic math facts of addition and subtraction before they move on to percentages. The same is true for these developmental stages.

As much as we might want to just skip a stage and order up some of the last stage, we can't. We need to *actually* develop. Also, like the math student, we have one dominant stage that we're currently in—we can't be in more than one stage at a time. The third-grade math student might be able to answer a couple of questions from fifth-grade math correctly, and they might also get a couple of questions from second-grade math wrong, but overall they're still at a third-grade math level.

But What about Them?

It's a question I routinely hear: "But if I'm adapting to another person, shouldn't they adapt to me too? Why should I have to change if they're not going to?" The sense I get from those who ask this is that they feel as though they are being asked to *give up* something, and if that's the case, others should be asked to give up something too. At the core, it's an issue of fairness for them.

In actuality, this type of adaptation doesn't require us to give up something or change who we are. When we adapt, we are able to use different strategies and approaches to be more effective in the moment at hand.

Essentially, we have more tools at our disposal. We've moved beyond the beginner do-it-yourselfer with just a hammer, a screwdriver, and a whole lot of repairs to do. In the fifth stage, it's as if we are now the professional contractor with a van full of tools, each specific to a particular task, and we know when and how to use them. As that contractor, when the job requires a specialized tool that I not only happen to have but also know how to use, I wouldn't think twice about using it. I also wouldn't feel as though it's unfair that the beginner just uses their hammer, or unfair that they won't do the job as well as I would.

Seeing things from a fifth-stage perspective doesn't mean we give up a part of ourselves or change who we are; it means we are able to see through both our filters and also the filters of others, and know how to Filter Shift in order to be more effective.

Moving Developmentally

Why don't we move through these stages more easily? Because we get stuck in the third stage. Developing the ability to Filter Shift is easier when we have greater clarity about where and how we typically get stuck. We need to see how we unknowingly promote ineffectiveness with each other, and how we tend to get stuck in a developmental quagmire. You'll likely recognize stories from each of these dynamics in the next two chapters.

• • • Key Points • • •

- Stage 1: Avoid or don't see even obvious differences
- Stage 2: Judge differences—I'm good and they're bad, or I'm bad and they're good
- Stage 3: Minimize the differences and focus on similarity
- Stage 4: See greater complexity of differences
- Stage 5: Adapt to that complexity

Chapter Seven

Reallusion and Stage 3

Her hair was dramatically spiked and dyed pink on the left side, clashing with her natural straight blonde hair on the right, in an obvious attempt at a hair fashion statement. She sat behind the reception counter of the hair salon in the mall looking young enough for this to be her first job.

This mall, in Sioux Falls, South Dakota, while small by most standards, had become the shopping mecca for many from the rural communities nearby. That was certainly the case for Miguel and myself. Early in our marriage, we lived close by in a Minnesota city of just ten thousand. During one of our trips to this mall, as we were strolling between shops, Miguel mentioned that he could use a haircut and wondered if he could actually get an appointment at a salon while we were there.

As a black man, Miguel has very tight kinky curls. At the time, his hairstyle of choice was a one-inch afro fade to about a half inch on the sides. On this particular trip to the mall, it had gotten a bit too long for him. He was ready for a cut.

When we walked into the salon at the mall, the young receptionist was visibly taken off guard. As Miguel approached her and asked if he could make an appointment to get his hair cut, her brows furrowed as she shook her head. "Oh, we don't cut black hair," she said calmly. Then abruptly, as if her own comment had startled her, she looked at me, gestured to my hair, and blurted, "I mean, we could dye your hair black and cut your hair. We just... don't cut...curly hair."

Even more self-startled by this second response, she barely let herself finish *that* statement when she corrected herself, again looking to me with desperation. "I mean, we could perm your hair and cut your hair, we just don't...you know..."

At this point, feeling a bit sorry for her and also worried about what might come out of her mouth next, we stopped her and said we understood. We'd look somewhere else, not to worry.

Sitting right in front of us, pink spikes and all, she was an example of the third-stage perspective: "a focus on differences divides, a focus on similarity unites." In this stage of minimizing differences, the strength is that we've gotten beyond seeing other groups as a threat, and we try to avoid denigrating or stereotyping others.

However, this is the last of the ineffective stages. Unfortunately, at roughly 70 percent, according to the IDI®, the majority of us are here. In fact, I frequently refer to it as the quagmire stage because it's where we tend to get stuck, both because it's a significant developmental step to move to the next stage, but also because we tend to endorse the attributes of this stage and thus promote its defining behaviors with each other. We often downplay the many ways we are different and instead focus on the few ways we are alike, making assumptions of similarity, many times unconsciously. We've learned in the second stage that looking at differences from a good/bad and us/them perspective isn't effective, so to counter that we pretend that we're *all* "us."

Remember chapter two about how we promote ineffectiveness with each other? All of those descriptions were from this third stage, which can manifest in a variety of ways.

Disliking Differentiation

The first time I noticed this phenomenon was at an HR conference at our local convention center. Miguel coincidentally was at the same convention center for a civil engineering event. On break between sessions in the expansive, bright corridor of the convention center talking to other attendees, I saw my husband walking toward me with three of his civil engineering colleagues from their suburban engineering office.

> We often downplay the many ways we are different and instead focus on the few ways we are alike, making assumptions of similarity, many times unconsciously. We've learned in the second stage that looking at differences from a good/bad and us/them perspective isn't effective, so to counter that we pretend that we're *all* "us."

The four of them looked as though they had, like middle school girls, called each other the night before to coordinate their outfits. This pack, however, was made up of middle-aged men all sporting khaki pants and light-blue dress shirts.

Except there was one glaring difference.

As you may know, the civil engineering profession is not a very diverse group. Currently, only 6.4 percent of registered civil engineers are black.[11] Miguel represented that disparity as the only black man in the group walking toward us. It was a situation that reminded me of the *Sesame Street* song, "One of these things is not like the other; one of these things just doesn't belong..."

I said to my fellow conference attendees, "Oh, there's my husband." When they asked which one, I knew I couldn't easily point him out by his clothes or his gender, so I said, "The black guy."

Can you guess how people respond when I point my husband out in this way when he's in a sea of white? The most typical response is nervous laughter. I can imagine what they're thinking might be, "Oh my God, she just said black! She's married to one and she doesn't know she's not supposed to say that!"

Just a few days ago I told this story during a presentation I was giving at a conference. One of the participants pulled me aside during a break and said, "I was really surprised you called your husband black. Why didn't you just say he was the second

---

11   "Employed persons by detailed occupation, sex, race, and Hispanic or Latino ethnicity." Current Population Survey, Bureau of Labor Statistics, U.S. Department of Labor, 2013. Retrieved from http://www.bls.gov/cps/cpsaat11.pdf

one from the left or the one with a darker blue shirt? Why did you have to point out his color?" So I told her about my flower test.

Last spring when I was with my daughter at a garden center picking out flowers to plant in our garden, I was trying to point out a flower that I really liked that happened to be a few aisles away. I pointed in the general direction and said, "I really like that one over there."

Just like my colleagues at the conference, my daughter asked, "Which one?"

The flower I was looking at was the only purple flower in a bed of red flowers, so I responded, "The purple one." It immediately reminded me of the story of pointing out my husband, and I realized the flower scenario could be a good litmus test. My daughter certainly didn't respond with nervous laughter saying, "Mom, you silly, you just said purple!"

If we don't feel uncomfortable pointing out the color of the purple flower, why do we feel uncomfortable pointing out the color of the black man? Again, it's because we have just transitioned from a second-stage perspective where pointing out a difference meant we were also assigning judgment. Purple flowers don't have a history of having negative judgments assigned to them, at least not that I know of. That's why we don't feel nervous saying the flower is purple.

That nervousness comes from our discomfort with pointing out differences, particularly when we're in the middle stage of development. If we think about that discomfort developmentally it makes sense. When we're in that third stage, we know we don't want to make sweeping judgments anymore so instead we focus on similarities. When a focus is placed on a difference—a *them*—

we assume there is a corresponding good/bad judgment attached to that difference. Since we don't want to judge good/bad, we'll pretend there is *no* us/them.

This is typically the case when the difference is one that has traditionally been marginalized, when the value that has been attached to the difference is somehow negative. Had I been pointing out one white man in a group of blacks, I don't think I would get the same discomfort if I had said, "The white guy," or "The structural engineer versus the geotechnical engineer."

There are also instances when the difference is irrelevant, when we aren't asked to differentiate, yet we point out the difference nonetheless. In these situations, it doesn't make sense to do so.

What's the Difference?

I encountered this recently in a conversation with another white woman. She was telling me about an experience she had at a retail store. Each time she talked about the clerk who helped her she described her as a short, little Asian woman.

After referring to her as such several times throughout the story, when she arrived at the punch line I was left hanging. The fact that this clerk was a short, little Asian woman had no relevance to the story at all. I kept searching for the connection to this difference she kept pointing out, but there wasn't any. In a case like this, the woman didn't need to differentiate the clerk by her race or size, yet she did anyway.

In the case of the conference where I was asked to pick out my husband—to differentiate—then we need to be comfortable doing so. But in situations where we aren't asked to differentiate, yet we do nonetheless, it can send very mixed and confusing signals.

My flower test is to think about the situation you are in as you're being asked to differentiate people. If you were in the same situation being asked to differentiate flowers, would you have a difficult time calling out the fact that the flower is purple? In addition, ask yourself if this is a situation where, like the short, little Asian woman, we're not asked to differentiate, so the distinction of purple is irrelevant.

This discomfort with differentiation keeps us from being our most effective because it discourages us from talking about the differences we see, even to the point of *pretending they aren't there*. It sets up a feeling of discomfort when differences are pointed out and at times even a discomfort with the differences themselves.

> This discomfort with differentiation keeps us from being our most effective because it discourages us from talking about the differences we see, even to the point of *pretending they aren't there.*

We *are* different. We have different approaches, perspectives, experiences. It's those differences that actually bring a richness to the workplace. If we are uncomfortable with them, if a nervous laugh pops out of us when the differences are mentioned, we aren't able to access the full breadth of that richness. In addition, the repeated minimization of difference works to further marginalize those who are different from the group norm, especially when their difference is a part of their identity and their leaders or coworkers proudly say they don't see it.

Reallusion

They wanted to get this right. After all, they were HR (Human Resources), and if anyone in their ad agency should be able to create a strong, diverse team it should be them. So when this group of about fifteen members struggled with hiring people of color on their own team, it was bothersome to them.

When I met with each of them individually, a few of them mentioned Cynthia, the one and only person of color on the team, as the problem. *She's not a team player; she's disrespectful; she doesn't care about us; she's actually quite rude.* Their argument for why they didn't have more people of color was essentially that it's too hard and why bother. They assumed all people of color would be just like they perceived Cynthia.

As a small team, they frequently had team parties. Every birthday and holiday was a reason to bring everyone together in a conference room to socialize around good food. It had become a part of their culture.

When I probed for specifics on how Cynthia was the problem, one of her colleagues claimed that Cynthia felt like she was too good for the rest of the team and that's why she wouldn't even go to these team gatherings. Another almost cried as she described her relationship with Cynthia, saying that she thought they got along well and she thought Cynthia liked her, but then Cynthia didn't even show up for her office birthday party, even after she had sent her a special invitation asking her to be sure to join the rest of the team. Cynthia didn't give a reason or even wish her happy birthday!

What her coworkers didn't understand was that, as a Jehovah's Witness, it was literally against Cynthia's religion to attend these celebrations. When I met with her, not only did she reveal this as the source of the issues her team had with her, but she also talked about how hurt she felt that her teammates continued to invite her to these celebrations *despite knowing* she was a Jehovah's Witness.

While presumably harboring the best of intentions, the team members were lost in a *reallusion*.

When this happens, we get distracted by the frames—the things we can easily see. In this case the frame was the behavior of not going to the team parties. We then subconsciously assume we attach the same filters—beliefs, perceptions, values—to that frame. We think we all share the same meaning around that frame, when in reality we don't.

Lost in a reallusion and assuming an absent similarity, if we identify a particular frame as rude, we assume it was *meant* to be rude. The only reason *I* wouldn't go to someone's birthday party would be if I didn't like them, didn't respect them, or just plain wanted to be mean to them. Therefore, if someone else doesn't come to my party, it *must* be for the same reasons.

We might look at Cynthia's situation from the outside and think we wouldn't have been fooled by such an "obvious" reallusion. Yet for most of us, this phenomenon of assuming similarity happens on a moment-by-moment basis. Because it happens unconsciously, it clouds how we experience our interactions and keeps us from seeing differences that may be at play.

In fact, many times when we make those split-second judgments—he's arrogant, she's mean, they're just lazy—we can't be sure about that judgment at all. We can *only* be sure that the judgment is a *reflection of the filters we attach to the frame of that behavior.* Read that statement again. It is the filter that pierces the reallusion; it is the filter that begins to make frames *visible;* it is the first step toward the fourth stage and an entirely new, effective perspective.

But we're not there yet.

That Sounds Racist

Another reason why it's difficult for us to move third-stage perspective into the first of the effective stages, Stage 4, is that we misidentify that fourth stage with the second stage. Thus, a move here is seen as regression instead of development.

Why?

Because the second and fourth stages have something in common, just as the first and third stages do. Specifically, it's their perspectives on difference. In the first and third stages, differences are either not seen or are minimized, while in the second and fourth they are outwardly addressed (see fig. 7.1). Individuals in both stages are typically very comfortable talking about differences. Of course the important difference between how they are addressed is that in the second stage it is only surface-level differences, and there is judgment placed on them. In the fourth stage, it is differences of greater complexity *without* that perspective of judgment.

To the eyes and ears of someone sitting in the middle of the stages, who has only personally experienced the second stage and is aware that they've developed out of it, they see and hear the fourth stage as synonymous with the second. That misidentification

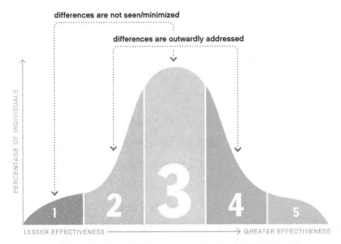

*Figure 7.1 The stages of development
and how we see and address differences.*

keeps them from moving forward, fearful of being misidentified themselves.

One of my local TV political correspondents experienced this firsthand when he did a story on funding for schools. He was speaking from a fourth-stage perspective, pointing out differences without judgment.

Specifically, he said that one of the reasons our schools need more funding today is the increase in immigrant populations. Today's immigrant students, he went on to explain, typically don't speak English and need additional services to teach them the language. They are also more often than not in need of free and reduced-price meals because they are low-income, their parents often don't know or understand the school system, and so they need additional resources to reach out to them.

These are comments that point out complexity of difference and are not placing a good/bad judgment. Immigrants are simply different.

Yet a number of viewers didn't hear it that way. From a third-stage perspective, they heard his commentary as judgmental, and the comments in social media reflected that. "He's a racist!" "He's anti-immigrant!"

When we are in the third stage trying to make the shift to the fourth, we hold ourselves back with those same messages in our head. *I don't want to offend anyone, so I'm not going to point out that difference.* With that decision we sink back into the comfort of the reallusion, our sight still obscured by automatic filters. The only way out is to start questioning our assumptions—ANY assumptions. "Is he *really* rude? How do I know? What *is* 'rude,' anyway?" In other words, we first need to SEE ourselves.

• • • Key Points • • •

- We tend to avoid pointing out differences because we still associate difference with good/bad and don't want to be perceived as judging.
- We tend to assume similarity: shared meaning or shared filters.
- We misidentify the fourth stage as the second stage, causing us to become mired in the third. Since the second stage is about recognizing differences, as is the fourth, we can easily see fourth-stage behavior as less developed and therefore not an appealing place to be or operate from.

Chapter Eight

Filter Shift #1
SEE Self: Acknowledge Our Filters

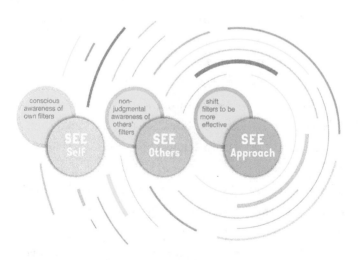

Figure 8.1. Filter Shift

Once we understand how our filters unknowingly decide for us and we have a sense of the stages of development, particularly where and how we get stuck, the natural next question is, so how do I become more effective?

For years, experts in our field of unconscious bias and cultural competence have said that we can be more effective, but that moving to that more effective stage takes approximately forty hours of intentional development work. That work essentially consists of examining different groups and the differences between them. Like many others, I followed that model for years, working with hundreds of groups across the country. Through that work, I began to see that as we helped people become aware of their unconscious filters, and moved them from the lower stages of effectiveness to the higher stages of effectiveness—particularly, from Stage 3 to Stage 4 and 5— there were key shifts that occurred for them in how they saw and responded to their filters.

Those shifts in how they saw and responded to their filters seemed consistent across groups, and they also seemed to be key developmental shifts. So I decided to experiment. I started to focus more specifically on teaching those developmental shifts.

That more targeted focus reduced the time it took individuals to develop from forty hours down to just nine. I have since refined that targeted focus to my Filter Shift approach. Each step of Filter Shift has key developmental shifts that happen, shifts that we home in on to become more effective and to reduce the negative impact of our filters (see fig. 8.1).

SEE: See, Explain, Evaluate

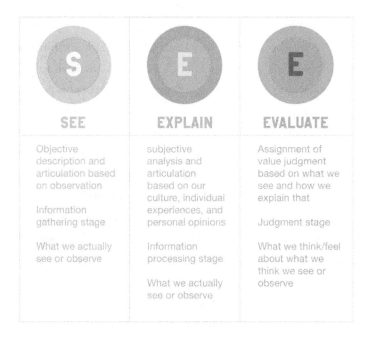

SEE	EXPLAIN	EVALUATE
Objective description and articulation based on observation	subjective analysis and articulation based on our culture, individual experiences, and personal opinions	Assignment of value judgment based on what we see and how we explain that
Information gathering stage		Judgment stage
What we actually see or observe	Information processing stage	What we think/feel about what we think we see or observe
	What we actually see or observe	

Figure 8.2. SEE helps us understand our three levels of observation: See, Explain, and Evaluate.

Remember our SEE acronym (see fig. 8.2)? The first level, *See*, is the only level not influenced by our filters. It is the level of objective information gathering and limited to only what we *actually* see. When we describe things at this level, we are describing the frames that we can easily see, but explaining them objectively.

The second level, *Explain*, adds the first layer of filters. It is more subjective based on our experiences, culture, and values, to name a few. This level is what we *think* we see or observe.

The final level, *Evaluate*, adds even more filters and judgment. It's how we *think* and *feel* about what we think we see.

What does it matter? The farther we move into the second and third levels of Explain and Evaluate, the more our filters are determining our thoughts and actions, the more likely the chance of misperception, and the less likely we'll be as effective as possible.

Unfortunately, in our moment-by-moment thinking, very few of our thoughts stop at the first level of SEE that isn't fueled by our filters. What do we do about it? Since there's no "off switch" for the other levels of observation, we need to learn how to work with them as we walk through the Filter Shift steps.

Basically, we move through our development in this progressive order. In individual situations, we walk through the situation, essentially creating a list of our thoughts to look first at our self, then others, and then our approach. Looking at that list we can see just how many of our thoughts aren't controlled by our filters and stop at just the first level of observation, See. (To see some examples of this, go to: FilterShift.com/Resources)

On a more complex level, each of these steps involves specific key developmental shifts that we need to understand and work through.

Filter Shift #1: SEE Self: Acknowledge Our Filters

If we were trying to teach a fish about the reality of air and land, I suspect the task would be a bit difficult. For the fish, these two very different realities would likely seem unimaginable because they would have nothing in their own experience or reality to which to tie those concepts. Asking a fish to believe in air and land is asking them to believe that other realities outside of their own exist. Since that requires too much of a leap, we'd likely start instead with what *is* real to them—water. We'd first have to help them see that they swim in water before we introduce the concepts of air and land.

The same is true for humans. In order to see and understand the reality of others, counter-intuitively, we need to first see our own reality and understand it as one of many realities. Since our reality comes from our own filters, we start by acknowledging our filters.

> In order to see and understand the reality of others, counter-intuitively, we need to first see our own reality and understand it as one of many realities. Since our reality comes from our own filters, we start by acknowledging our filters.

Essentially, the process of acknowledging our filters is a process of being conscious of what is typically unconscious for us. That seems like an impossible task, but fortunately we have a conscious link to our unconscious filters—our expectations. Formed by our filters, our expectations make predictions for us of how others will operate. But, as we know, those predictions aren't always right. By now you can probably guess why—because our filters are different from the person who isn't meeting our expectations.

That's how situations of unmet expectations can become valuable opportunities for us. They remind us that different filters are at play and become a chance to stop and examine our own filters, as well as the filters of others, in direct relation to the situation.

(For an activity on how to detail your expectations and separate your frames from your filters: FilterShift.com/Resources)

When we expose our own filters by bringing them to the conscious level, we can begin to see them more objectively. That in turn allows us to see the filters of others more objectively. In order to acknowledge our filters, specific shifts need to occur:

- Shift from subconscious right and wrong to personal accountability
- Shift from bias is bad, to bias is human
    a. From I don't have favorites in people to I have preferences in approach
    b. From perpetuating fallacy to attaining awareness
    c. From unknowingly offending to being able to predict reactions

Shift from Subconscious Right and Wrong to Personal Accountability

There is one particular (two-part) question that I hear frequently after explaining the stages of development, specifically the last stage of adapting our behavior: "Why do *I* need to change my behavior? Shouldn't the other person have to change theirs too?"

The sense I get from people posing this question is that they feel as though they are being asked to give up something, and, if that's the case, others should be asked to give up something too. At heart, they think it's not fair. But we don't need to give up anything or change who we are to be more effective. Think back to our example of the do-it-yourselfer with two tools and the contractor with a van full of tools. If using a new tool—or a new filter—helps us to be more effective in the situation, then why not use it?

It's more difficult than just picking up a different tool out of a toolbox because interactions happen on a two-way street and we think, "Well, if I have to change, they should have to change too!" But if I were actually driving down a two-way street and the driver approaching me was oblivious to a multitude of road hazards between us, would I feel as though I should be blind to them too? This shift is about accountability. When we operate in the stages of lower effectiveness on the left side of the developmental continuum, we choose our responses—or at least our filters choose our responses—with a goal of being right, good, or professional. When we operate on the right side, we see and understand that it's not about being right, good, or professional, but about being more effective.

On the left side, it is our filters that decide how we respond. Since that decision-making process happens unconsciously, we aren't aware of the fact that there are other options. Acknowledging that our filters make decisions for us allows us the space to consider other possibilities—both in how we could see and experience the situation, as well as how others might be seeing and experiencing it.

Shift from Bias Is Bad to Bias Is Human

I was once told that years ago there was a special exhibit at the Smithsonian Museum about prejudice. When you approached the exhibit entrance there were two large wooden doors set a few feet apart from each other. Above the left door was a sign that read "For those that are prejudiced." Above the right door a sign read "For those that are not prejudiced." The door on the right was a false door. Those who tried to enter couldn't. The message was clear—*we all have prejudice*. In order to understand and eliminate it, we need to first admit that we have it.

Call it prejudice or call it the more common word we use today, bias; in either case, it's seen as something bad. If you say that I'm biased then you're also saying that I'm racist or sexist or homophobic. Bias is equated with both extreme behavior and negative intent. It's certainly not something to aspire to having. So of course I don't have it. My behavior isn't extreme and my intent is always positive. I'm not biased.

The reality is we are all biased thanks to our filters. They *create* our bias. If we don't want to admit we have bias, we won't be able to acknowledge our filters.

> We need to move the discussion about bias out of the realm of blame and shame. It's something all of our brains do. When we accept that, we can approach awareness of our biases more openly.

We need to move the discussion about bias out of the realm of blame and shame. It's something all of our brains do. When we accept that, we can approach awareness of our biases more openly. We then become more aware of the drivers of the second and third levels of observation: our culture, experiences, values, and beliefs. Only when we are fully aware of how these drivers control our perceptions and misperceptions are we able to stop them when they get in the way.

It helps to begin thinking about bias as something that is not only the purview of racists but instead as something endemic to all of us.

From I Don't Have Favorites in People to I Have Preferences in Approach

No, of course I don't have a favorite employee. That would just be wrong! As I say this, I'm actually visibly favoring one employee over another. But since we know that having a favorite is bad, of course I don't have one.

We say that consciously while our filters are working away unconsciously to determine who is our favorite.

When we acknowledge our filters—first we have to be aware of them—we can then acknowledge that we are clearly seeing what our preferences are. I know that in general I tend to look more favorably at people who, like me, are extroverted and emotionally expressive. When I acknowledge that versus shove it under the rug, I take power away from that bias.

I'm also able to see it from the perspective of a preference in approach versus a favoring of a specific person. Eventually, then, I'll be able to see that different circumstances call for different approaches, and my preferences will change accordingly.

From Perpetuating Fallacy to Attaining Awareness

The vast majority of us think we are much more competent than we actually are. If we all agree that bias is bad and we think that we are good, it's easy to come to the conclusion "I don't have bias."

It's *not possible* for us to be unbiased. Our unconscious optometrist is going to keep prescribing filters; we will continue to have preferences. Therefore, to set out eliminating bias as a goal continues to perpetuate the fallacy that it is attainable, and also continues to encourage us to pretend we don't have bias. Being nonjudgmental, however, *is* attainable. It is possible to first be aware of our biases and then build the skill of holding them in check and questioning them to the point that we can hold all options as equally viable.

From Unknowingly Offending to
Being Able to Predict Reactions

When we try to pretend that we don't have bias, our bias ends up in control. And when our bias is in control, we many times don't know when, or even if, we have offended someone. When we move to the right side of the developmental continuum, we are more aware of our filters and how they are impacting the situation, our perception, and even how others may perceive their own filters. Once we have a sense of the filters of others, we can more easily predict how they will respond in a situation.

• • • Key Points • • •

- Filter Shift is SEE Self, SEE Others, SEE Approach. The SEE in each step is our levels of observation: See, Explain, Evaluate. Only the first level is objective; the second two levels are influenced by our filters.

- Key developmental shifts take place between the first three stages of lesser effectiveness and the last two stages of greater effectiveness on the developmental spectrum. The Filter Shift approach focuses on those key developmental shifts.

- The first Filter Shift is SEE Self: Acknowledge Our Filters. In this step we bring our filters to the conscious level.

- The two key developmental shifts are:

o   Shift from subconscious right and wrong to personal accountability. Acknowledging our filters and the power they have in making decisions for us helps us consider other possibilities, and also helps us to accept responsibility for those decisions.

o   Shift from bias is bad, to bias is human. We are all biased and our biases are formed by our filters.

◊   Shift from having favorites in people to having a preference in approach, all while fully considering other approaches without judgment.

◊   Shift from perpetuating fallacy to attainable awareness. It isn't possible to eliminate our bias or our filters, but being nonjudgmental is attainable.

◊   Shift from unknowingly offending to being able to predict reactions. When we are more aware of the filters involved in a situation, we are more able to predict reactions.

Chapter Nine

Filter Shift #2
SEE Others: Assume Difference

Question Our Filters

After back-to-back business trips to the South, I became hyper-attentive trying to identify all the layers of difference between that region and the Midwest where I live.

There were the differences that were easy to see—the frames—like grits at the hotel breakfast or BBQ pork with pancakes at the conference lunch buffet. There were also some differences that weren't as obvious—the filters. There was the Southern hospitality and the fact that, on both trips, my clients took me out to dinner—something that rarely if ever happens in other parts of the country. There was the formality, as I was referred to as "Ms. Taylor" and "ma'am" more often than I was referred to as Sara.

Then there were the two men at the airport that my filters misidentified. In just a split-second glance at the first man in an airport restaurant, I saw his tailored suit, shined shoes, white skin, and gray hair. Within milliseconds, my filters subconsciously told me with full certainty that he was a self-absorbed, rich, white, American businessman. A few minutes later, I heard him on the phone and realized he was speaking Arabic—clearly his native tongue.

My filter about his nationality was wrong.

We exchanged a couple of commentaries about the news broadcast on the screen in front of us as we ate. I left to go catch my flight, and as I boarded I noticed him already seated on the same plane a few rows behind me. He saw me struggling to retract the stuck handle of my carry-on bag and actually jumped up from his seat, rows away, to come and help me. Once again, my filter—this time that he was self-absorbed—was wrong.

When I finally take my seat it's next to another white man, this one in casual clothes with a scruffy beard. Once again my brain makes an immediate classification. I put him in the category of a techie on a business trip that's not going to be very friendly or want a conversation. Turns out he was a very warm and friendly Englishman on holiday.

Once again, my assumptions were wrong. My filters had misidentified what I was seeing and passed along an incorrect judgment to my conscious mind.

As I sat there in conversation with the Englishman, it struck me that difference was all around me. I needed to start with the belief that my assumptions were incorrect. I needed to constantly challenge my filters and assume that what I was seeing differed from what my filters were telling me.

It's easy to do at an airport, in a roomful of strangers, or when we're traveling to new places, but it's not a natural tendency to assume difference in our daily routine, in moment-by-moment situations. When we're interacting with the cashier at the local coffee shop, when we're in a meeting with others from our same work team, when we see someone we might think we have a kinship with—*that* is when we also have to assume difference.

> This hyper-attentiveness to difference comes more naturally when we're placed in new settings, but our challenge is to make that level of attentiveness our default mode in every situation.

We need to start with the knowledge that *we are vastly different*.

This hyper-attentiveness to difference comes more naturally when we're placed in new settings, but our challenge is to make that level of attentiveness our default mode in every situation.

See Difference in Similarity (or Look for Complexity in Homogeneity)

Once again, back to Cheryl, who started to see complexity where she formerly saw homogeneity. She identified the fact that the frames were similar, the things she could easily see like skin color, geography, socio-economic level—things we typically look at to identify a difference (if we don't easily see difference at this level, we think we're alike). Then she started to see the differences at the level of filters, the level with greater complexity and impact. In addition, where her filters used to look at the similarity of frame and assume similarity of filters, now she understands that regardless of frame similarity, the filters differ.

The Four Specific Components of Filter #2: Shift of Assume Difference

1. Shift from the Golden Filter to the Platinum Filter
2. Shift from Inability and Discomfort with Differentiating to Ability and Comfort
3. Shift from the Minimizing Mantra to the Acknowledging Mantra
4. Shift from Broad Brushstrokes to Complex Differentiation

Shift from the Golden Filter to the Platinum Filter

We saw how the Golden Filter served Bill Richardson—it didn't. The negative consequences of operating with this mindset are obvious when we look retrospectively at someone else's mishap. However, they aren't always as clear for us on a day-to-day basis.

Like Richardson, we aren't as effective as we'd like to be, because we are assuming similarity. But our interactions aren't with a dictator that can throw us out of his office or threaten our lives. That's why the consequences of operating with the Golden Filter aren't nearly as obvious for us.

People will argue that the basic principle of the Golden Filter is admirable.

Yes, the Golden Filter is admirable—especially if the alternative is to treat others poorly, discriminate, or just plain be mean. Luckily, we have another alternative: treat others as *they* would like to be treated, the Platinum Filter. Since our filters determine only how *we* want to be treated, when we operate with the Golden Filter and treat others the same, we are essentially assuming others are operating with the same filters; we've fallen victim to the reallusion.

The Platinum Filter assumes difference. I ask myself what filters others are looking through to see the situation, then respond accordingly.

Let's go back to the parent/teacher conference and how our teacher, Becky, could have responded differently to be more effective. Had she followed the SEE model, she would have understood that her own filters created the response of restraining her emotions. She would have also understood that the mother's filters created the response of expressing her emotions.

If she had been operating with the Platinum Filter, her response would have acknowledged the mother's filters, not her own.

That would have sounded something like, "It sounds as though you really care about your daughter's grades. I do too. She's definitely capable of doing better. I have some ideas about what each of us can do to help her. Let's talk about it."

That response would likely have garnered her the mother's respect. That response would have made the situation better. That response was a platinum response.

Shift from Inability and Discomfort with Differentiating to Ability and Comfort

With this shift, we first need to become comfortable. We're not talking about a comfort with the difference itself, because many of us are comfortable with differences to a certain extent. What we need to become more comfortable with is *talking about those differences* when the situation calls for it. Actually pointing them out when it's pertinent. That's what we're able to do in the acknowledging fourth stage. That's what my local political correspondent did with his story on immigrants in the schools.

Referring back to the Development Continuum:

- In *Stage 2*, I point out differences and judge them good or bad.
- In *Stage 3*, I don't want to point out differences because people might think that I'm judging.
- In *Stage 4*, I point out differences without judging and can start to see complexity—that's when I'm ready to start becoming more effective.

That effectiveness means seeing greater complexity in the differences, specifically, moving beyond seeing the differences in frame that are easy to identify, and better understanding the differences in filters that most of us have a more difficult time seeing.

A marketing campaign for a multi-state healthcare system I work with illustrates this capability. Over time, more and more Latinos were moving into the communities they served, but few of those Latinos were using these specific clinics. So the organization decided they wanted to begin marketing to Latinos.

They did what most organizations would do in that situation—translated their current materials into Spanish and changed the patient pictures on the front from white patients to Latino patients. Both of those were changes in the differences that are easy to identify, the frames.

The campaign failed and they couldn't understand why. They had created great-looking brochures with proper translation and placed them in strategic locations in the community where they thought Latinos were sure to encounter them. They had also stayed consistent with the important key messages found in all of their literature about quality healthcare and support for families.

It wasn't until they began to understand the filters Latinos may be looking through that they realized the reality that Latinos see health differently, see care differently, see support differently, and see families differently. The way the campaign addressed each of these concepts in the marketing materials needed to be through those different filters.

When they looked at this more complex differentiation and Filter Shifted, they were able to completely change their messaging to Latinos and create more effective marketing.

Shift from the Minimizing Mantra to the Acknowledging Mantra

"A focus on differences divides; a focus on similarities unites." This is the mantra that we live by in the third stage. It keeps us stuck assuming similarity instead of assuming difference.

The fourth-stage Acknowledging Mantra is, "I see complexity and I don't judge it." We're only able to live by this mantra once we're able to see how others perceive situations through their filters, and understand those filters as not good or bad, just different. This new perspective opens up more possibilities, not only in how we understand others, but in our own responses as well. This leads us to a second Acknowledging Mantra, "Bring it on! The more differences the better!"

Shift from Broad Brushstrokes to Complex Differentiation

When we see the difference between the broad brushstrokes and the pointillism painting, we see more complex differentiation. We see more of what is actually influencing a situation. We also have a greater richness of experiences available to us.

• • • Key Points • • •

- The second Filter Shift is SEE Others: Assume Difference—instead of assuming similarity, we assume difference.
- The key developmental shifts happening with this second step are shifts to:
    - The Platinum Rule: This acknowledges that others, operating with different filters, will likely want to be treated differently than we want to be treated.
    - A Comfort with Differentiating: I'm comfortable pointing out differences because I see the greater complexity, and I do so without judging.

- o The Acknowledging Mantra: I see complexity and I don't judge it.
- o Complex Differentiation: I have the ability to see greater complexity.

Chapter Ten

Filter Shift #3:
SEE Approach: Detach Filters

My Spaghetti

My mother-in-law, Zoila, had been living with us for a few months. By that point the novelty had worn off and the stress of sharing our home was starting to rise.

She had indefinitely extended her visit from the Dominican Republic following a fateful afternoon when the doctors told us she had Stage III breast cancer. Her treatment was aggressive with both chemotherapy and radiation. She was sick and our house was a stressful place. Between trying to care for her (along with our three young kids) and balance full-time jobs, my husband and I were having a tough time keeping up with everything.

Because I had a little more flexibility in my job, it was also up to me to get her to almost daily appointments in the middle of my own work schedule.

One evening, amidst the chaos of making dinner, starting the bath and bedtime routine, and simultaneously checking the kids' homework, mother-in-law meds, and work emails, my husband Miguel mouths to me from across the room with exaggerated lips, "We have to talk."

As he pulls me aside Miguel whispers, "Mom really doesn't like your spaghetti. I don't think you should make it anymore."

Now is when I should probably insert some sort of a disclaimer about my behavior because I'm not proud of my response. Yes, I was stressed, but what most influenced my self-centered reaction was my filters. At the time I didn't understand them, so my filters had free rein. In fact, I'd like to think that it was my filters and not me that responded in that moment.

I didn't acknowledge her sickness. I didn't think about how awful it would be for someone who is so ill to have to eat anything I cook, much less my spaghetti from a jar. Instead, all I could say was, "If she can't come to me and tell me to my face that she doesn't like my spaghetti, then the problem doesn't exist!" And I probably said it with jutting chin, pursed lips, and sassy neck swaying.

It's not that I was particularly attached to my spaghetti. Like everyone else in my family, I too suffered through my jar-dumping, box-opening style of cooking that I relied on at the time. I just couldn't believe that she was going to my husband to complain.

And that's how I saw it—a whiny complaint. From the view through my filters, she didn't really want to resolve the issue. If she did, she would have come directly to me and talked to me about the problem. We'd discuss it calmly and then work toward a resolution. When she instead went to my husband, well, that could only mean she was just whining and complaining. If she really wanted to resolve things, she would have come to me.

So I waited.

I waited for her to approach me directly so I could figure out what she did like to eat. As far as I was concerned, the ball was in her court because *she* was the one with the problem. And I waited. She didn't come to me and I was getting more and more bothered by the situation. After all, this was my family and my home. I didn't want conflict in our midst. I was bothered enough that I wanted to talk with someone about it, someone who could help me figure out if I was wrong in waiting for her to talk to me.

Who did I consult? I didn't consult another Dominican woman like Zoila, who might share her perspective and give me some insight. No, I talked to someone just like me. Carolyn, my college roommate, is another white woman who grew up in small-town Minnesota. I knew she shared my perspective.

After I relayed the situation and my response to it, I got the gratification I needed as she said, "You are so right! I say that all the time. If you can't tell me directly what's wrong, how am I

> **I realize it wasn't the situation itself, it was our filters that got in the way.**

supposed to know?" Score one for me. I was right. My mother-in-law was wrong.

I don't remember what happened next or if I ever made my spaghetti again, but I do remember that one minor situation didn't help our relationship. As I reflect now, I realize it wasn't the situation itself, it was our filters that got in the way. Zoila was an indirect communicator. That was her frame, the behavior I could easily see.

Unfortunately, I couldn't see that frame without bias because I could only see it through my filters. Those filters were telling me that there was only one way to communicate respectfully and that was to be direct. Frame: direct communication. Filter attached to that frame: respect. When I saw the opposite frame of indirect communication, I automatically assumed it had the opposite filter attached to it. For me, indirect communication meant Zoila was disrespecting me.

In actuality, when she communicated indirectly through Miguel she did so because she respected me too much to tell me to my face. For her, direct communication was disrespectful.

We were both products of our cultures.

I grew up with my mother telling me to stop whining when I went to her with a complaint about my brother. "Talk to him yourself." The message was clear: If the problem is between the two of you, don't involve me; deal with it yourself. In the work world, I was told over and over again that it was company policy to handle any conflicts respectfully by going directly to the individual involved.

Zoila was taught much the opposite. She was encouraged to use a third party as a mediator or, if you end up in a face-to-face discussion, use stories and metaphors to more softly and respectfully address the conflict.

Zoila isn't alone. In fact, the vast majority of the world teaches and prefers the indirect style. For them it is a frame: indirect communication. Filter attached to that frame: respect.

The problem is that this attachment of certain frames to specific filters happens unconsciously. We aren't aware of the fact that our unconscious mind makes these decisions. A judgment is made and the case is closed before it's sent to our conscious mind. Those decisions and judgments are based on and confirm our past experiences, which is why we trust them. Certain behaviors are good, right, or professional and others are bad, wrong, or unprofessional. The frame is solidly attached to the filter.

But because we don't all have the same past experiences, we aren't all making the same decisions and judgments in our unconscious minds.

In order to make the decisions consciously, we need to be able to detach our filters from our frames. I needed to see that my frame wasn't and isn't the only option for respectful communication. It's just one

> **In order to make the decisions consciously, we need to be able to detach our filters from our frames.**

option. Once I realize this, I am then able to see through the filters of others without judgment, and my filter of respect is free to be attached to other very different frames. I am able to see that Zoila's opposing frame of indirect communication is actually attached to the filter of respect.

While spaghetti-fueled conflicts may come along once in a lifetime, our ability to detach our frames and filters is tested on a moment-by-moment basis. Only when we are able to do this are we able to approach each of those moments more effectively.

Three Reminders

A reminder of three key concepts to help us detach filters from frames:

1. **Assume positive intent:** If the behavior we see is one we don't like, we typically assume there was negative intent behind it. "They're so rude." "How could they be so disrespectful?" "That was really unprofessional." If we instead assume they had positive intent and, like me, were trying to connect in a productive way, then we allow a space for a different filter to be attached to the frame.

2. **Shift from past experiences deciding for us to relativity of current situation:** When our filters and frames are firmly attached, since our filters are formed by our past experiences, we are allowing those past experiences to dictate the situation for us when they may not be relevant at all. If we focus on the current situation and only the context surrounding it, we can reduce the impact of those past experiences deciding for us.

3. **Filters and behaviors are relative:** We've heard it before but it's difficult to actually believe: it's all relative. I need to remind myself that each person's behaviors are relative

to them, not to me—that they are formed by their filters, not mine.

(For an activity that helps us detach our filters: FilterShift. com/Resources)

Adapting and Compromise: 3 Key Questions and 3 Steps

Let's take a look at that last step in the SEE Framework, SEE Approach. This last step is about adapting our behavior to be more effective. How do we do that? We mind the gap. We pay attention to the difference between our behavior and the behavior of others, and consider bridging that gap by asking three key questions of ourselves:

1. **Am I capable**? Do I understand the intended values behind the behavior I am going to adapt to, and am I actually able to exhibit that sincerely without judgment?

2. **Am I comfortable**? Do I understand the behavior well enough that I feel comfortable adapting?

3. **What are the consequences**? Have I considered the consequences? If there is significant risk involved and this is my first time adapting to this behavior, the consequences might be too high.

Keep in mind that adapting is a conscious choice. There may be situations when we aren't capable, comfortable, or the consequences are too high. In those situations, we shouldn't change our behavior, but we should still try to learn from the interaction.

Specifically, we can compromise by honoring both approaches. When we do so we:

1. **Still use personal preference**: preferred behavior or style.
2. **Identify the difference**: specifically, SEE the different behavior or style objectively without Explanation, Evaluation, or Judgment.
3. **Outwardly acknowledge** the difference and shared positive intent.

If I am compromising in order to mind the gap with someone that is expressive while I am restrained, I'll continue to use my preferred style and restrain my emotion, but I'll also look at the expressive style objectively and remember that their opposing behaviors are a reflection of the same values and intent that I hold, although I exhibit the opposite behaviors.

I also need to keep in mind how they might perceive the fact that I'm not expressing my emotion as much as they are and, particularly, that this might seem untrustworthy to them. Finally, I will acknowledge the difference and express our shared positive intent. That might sound something like, "I see that you really care about this issue. I do too. I don't typically express my emotions outwardly, but know that I care deeply about this as well. I know we both want to resolve this, so let's see what we can figure out together."

(To see an example of how Becky the student teacher could have followed these steps to compromise: FilterShift.com/Resources)

• • • Key Points • • •

- We tend to unconsciously attach certain frames to specific filters. Certain behaviors are good, right, or professional and others are bad, wrong, or unprofessional. To make decisions more consciously and be more effective, we need to detach those filters from the frames.

- Three reminders help us to detach filters:
  - **Assume positive intent:** If my filter tells me someone else was disrespectful and I assume positive intent, then I need to consider that they are operating with a different filter.

  - **Shift from past experiences deciding for us:** Since our filters are formed by our past experiences, when we detach our filters we're also shifting from those past experiences making decisions for us.

  - **Filters and behaviors are relative:** Each person's behaviors are relative to them, not to me; they are dictated by their filters, not mine.

- Three key questions to answer to learn if I am ready to adapt: Am I capable? Am I comfortable? And what are the consequences?

- If the answer is "no" to any of those, then compromise with three key steps: Use preference; identify the difference; outwardly acknowledge the difference and shared positive intent.

Chapter Eleven

Conclusion—Filters Shifted

So what does it look like? How do you actually operate differently when you've learned to Filter Shift? I posed these and other questions to a few of my clients and they've been gracious enough to share their thoughts, but not all of their legal teams agreed with their generosity, so we had to list those as anonymous.

How do you see, think, and operate differently now that you are able to Filter Shift?

"I'm more aware of who I am and how I initially react to almost every situation. I try to be aware of my filters, how they might affect my reaction, and how I might exchange an immediate reaction for a more thoughtful, adjusted one. I used to have a strong focus on treating everyone as equal, which often resulted in internal conflict. I couldn't really get my arms around why I felt that way. Now I get that everyone is different and comes from different places, and thus has different needs and filters. Not just race or culture differences, but differences in priorities, values, needs, ideas, upbringing—everything different. To have meaningful relationships and interactions requires different approaches, and I'm now much more likely to adjust my approach to match what the person across from me needs, instead of trying to treat everyone equally. I'm much more comfortable not feeling like I need to treat everyone the same. I now respond differently in almost every situation. When I don't, it's usually because I've missed an unconscious bias or let one of my filters dictate my reaction." —Anonymous

> To have meaningful relationships and interactions requires different approaches, and I'm now much more likely to adjust my approach to match what the person across from me needs, instead of trying to treat everyone equally.

"I work in HR and help coach managers through tough employee issues. In EVERY employee issue that is raised to me, the first thing I do after listening to the situations and/or concerns is walk through the Filter Shift framework in my head, and then I help the managers I am supporting walk through it as well. It's so easy to jump to the wrong conclusions or paths to action when managing employee performance, so this framework helps me step back before action and makes sure we're not explaining and

> This framework helps me step back before action and makes sure we're not explaining and interpreting the behaviors we are seeing through our own biased filters.

interpreting the behaviors we are seeing through our own biased filters. This isn't something I did consistently before this development, and I know I went down some ineffective paths as a result." —Chris Matuseski, Director of Organizational Effectiveness for a healthcare organization

"*See the gold* is a phrase I like to use when I describe what it means to be able to Filter Shift. When we are able to recognize bias and identify how it can impact our perceptions of others, only then can we see people for who they really are. I proudly look for the gold in everyone I meet, and this helps me to connect with people naturally, to lead, to influence, to negotiate, or simply befriend people whom I share nothing (in common) with. I am less entrenched in my own thought processes on a number of issues. One that comes to mind is politics. I think this work has actually helped me to be less judgmental of the other side, understand their perspective, and know you cannot change someone's deeply held beliefs, but you *can* compromise." —Namita Eveloy, deepSEE Consulting

"My awareness of subtle but poignant different perspectives has increased dramatically. I feel less tentative in facing emotionally charged situations by being more transparent and taking more time trying to understand how actions and contexts are perceived by others based on 'where they are coming from.' I feel less judgmental of others' behaviors by seeing them as developmental rather than 'appropriate' or not." —Executive leader, government agency

"One of the most important differences about how I respond in every situation is the awareness of my own filters and preferences. I have always tried to be as inclusive a person as possible, but until developing in my own ability to Filter Shift, I viewed inclusion as simply being respectful of others' unique identities. Now I have a deep understanding of my own identity, which allows me to understand even more fully the complexity of others—as well as home in on the moments when my filters may be causing conflict." —Anonymous

> Now I have a deep understanding of my own identity, which allows me to understand even more fully the complexity of others—as well as home in on the moments when my filters may be causing conflict.

"The ability to more reliably recognize how my decisions and actions take place in a (multi)cultural context empowers me to more skillfully adapt my behavior and words to account for differences. Being a part of the majority culture, it can be easy to assume that others share a similar perspective and culture and underestimate how commonly my own preconceptions, biases, and stereotypes can obstruct effective cross-cultural communication. Developing the ability to Filter Shift affirms how important it is to know yourself, how you are influenced by your own cultural norms, and how those norms are not universally shared or expressed in the same way. This one insight alone is helpful in reflecting on experiences, and encourages learning to adapt both what and how we express ourselves in words and actions more effectively in a multicultural setting (and we are nearly always operating in a multicultural setting)." —Anonymous

"I pick up on subtle cues from people more effectively. Whether it is while facilitating a meeting, conducting a training, or participating in a brainstorm, I have a keen sense of how to 'make space' for diverse voices to be heard and respected. I've learned to 'tune in' to subtlety in body language and in communication, and to approach the situations with humility. I've learned how to engage more effectively to get to know people on a more personal level, without being intimidated or distant because of difference." —Marie Logsden, Planned Parenthood of the Rocky Mountains

"I view diversity as more than cultural/ethnic influences now. I realize that being effective as I interact across difference involves a lot more, and to be a successful communicator you must understand where people are so you can effectively reach them. I have a wider perspective of seeing and thinking about differences, not only with ethnic/cultural/religious affects, but also with beliefs and understanding of others and accepting them for who they are." —Carol Chong, Alliance for a Healthier Generation

Describe something that surprised you or an "Aha!" moment as you learned to Filter Shift.

"Many people, even supposed experts in the field, operate and speak from the left side (of the developmental continuum). As a result, we often misunderstand that minimizing differences is the 'politically correct' way we should think, talk, and behave.

> **This paradigm was freeing and eye-opening.**

This paradigm was freeing and eye-opening. I loved the phrase 'differences that make a difference' because I think it brings clarity to an otherwise really confusing landscape. I use and think of that phrase ALL THE TIME!" —Anonymous

"As an HR professional, I've had a number of surprise insights or 'aha' moments that helped me better recognize and adapt to address how unconscious bias creates (and sustains) artificial barriers to recruiting, selecting, and retaining a more diverse and inclusive workforce. I now have a greater appreciation for how applicants from different cultural backgrounds or abilities (such as someone on the autism spectrum) might experience bias at different stages in the hiring process, and how that hidden bias operates to keep us from hiring and retaining some exceptional candidates." —Anonymous

As an HR professional, I've had a number of surprise insights or 'aha' moments that helped me better recognize and adapt to address how unconscious bias creates (and sustains) artificial barriers to recruiting, selecting, and retaining a more diverse and inclusive workforce.

"I have learned that the Filter Shift process is about being humble and vulnerable, caring a lot about learning, caring a lot about people, and listening. It does require a sense of confidence to take what you hear and see, and then adjust. I think the anxiety of making a mistake often causes professionals—even highly perceptive people—to shy away from acting when they see that something is off. The experience we went through to learn how to Filter Shift helped me understand how to pick up on the moments where adjustment is important, and also gave me the confidence to act." —Marie Logsden, Planned Parenthood of the Rocky Mountains

What would you tell others who are debating whether they should develop their ability to Filter Shift?

"It's not a quick fix. You need to continue to make an effort to move from your current stage to more meaningful stages. Just do it!" —Anonymous

> ...but for me it has been deeply significant in my ability to more fully live into a better version of myself while encouraging and emboldening others to do the same . . . at the same time . . . in the same room.

"Do it! On *so, so, so* many levels it is transformative, but for me it has been deeply significant in my ability to more fully live into a better version of myself while encouraging and emboldening others to do the same . . . at the same time . . . in the same room. It's been spiritual. The great commandment: Love the Lord your God with all your heart, mind, soul, and strength, AND love your neighbor as yourself. I've spent most of my faith energy in formally studying and practicing 'loving God,' and this gives me a framework for 'loving thy neighbor as thyself'. . . especially if how I desire to be loved is on my own terms—then I'm required to love others on their own terms. (Go Platinum!) Do this. If for no other reason—to better know thyself." —Chad Schwitters, Executive Director, Urban Homeworks

"If you're serious about improving your ability to interact across difference and willing to admit you have room for improvement, you will undoubtedly learn some things about yourself. Understanding where your filters are rooted and how to recognize the effect they're having will help you more effectively match your approach to what the needs of your audience are. It's worth it!" —Anonymous

"Filter Shift has helped me to develop a critical level of EQ, to be able to be more effective bridging differences in a multitude of settings. I am quickly able to see filters and able to connect with people I would never have been able to connect with as I see the rationale that props up their behaviors. This is a fundamental skill in today's world. I would ask them to consider an ongoing tension or conflict in their lives, and ask if they are ready to take the first step to resolving it. Understanding differing values is powerful, and it will redefine how you communicate, negotiate, and come across to others." —Namita Eveloy, deepSEE Consulting

> I am quickly able to see filters and able to connect with people I would never have been able to connect with as I see the rationale that props up their behaviors. This is a fundamental skill in today's world.

"I think that once you describe to someone the full array of factors that contribute to their unique and complex identity, folks are more willing to engage in seeing others without judgment. When you realize that you want to be honored for all the intricate things that create your identity, it becomes much harder not to honor another's identity as well." —Anonymous

"Policy makers need to look beyond compliance to the competitive advantage of having a diverse and inclusive workforce.

Without the ability to Filter Shift, organizations are unlikely to enjoy that competitive advantage. It takes knowledge, skill, and practice to realize the advantages of having a diverse and inclusive workforce." —Anonymous

"This is THE MOST IMPORTANT work an organization and individuals can be doing to achieve their mission and/or maintain effectiveness as a company. Having done this critical work, it's easy to see how without it, an organization risks becoming irrelevant very quickly in an ever-changing world." — Chris Matuseski, Director of Organizational Effectiveness for a healthcare organization

> This is THE MOST IMPORTANT work an organization and individuals can be doing to achieve their mission and/or maintain effectiveness as a company.

"You must do the hard work. It is your responsibility to learn, to listen, and to stay curious, humble, and engaged. This is not a one-time read or a quick training. It's a long-term process. You have to engage and you have to prioritize the learning. You have to care and you have to invest. Values need to align with resources. I think it is nearly impossible for any organization in any industry to argue the value of cultural competence in this age of globalization. However, I think too many organizations ascribe to the value and fail to assign the resources. This misalignment is a barrier to success and ultimately discourages talent, consumers, creativity, and the potential for successful programs, sales, or services." —Marie Logsden, Planned Parenthood of the Rocky Mountains

About the Author

Sara Taylor is the president and founder of deepSEE Consulting. She is a nationally recognized speaker and consultant specializing in the areas of leadership, diversity, and organizational effectiveness. She and her husband, Miguel, have four kids and live outside of St. Paul, Minnesota.

Acknowledgments

This book has been in the making for at least a decade and is a result of my work throughout my career. During that time, I have had the opportunity to work with, learn from, and be inspired by so many wonderful people. As such, I have many to thank.

I want to start by thanking all the wonderful teachers from grade school to graduate school that have not only instructed but also inspired me. I especially want to thank my English and writing teachers. Barbara Fosheim, I still hear your voice as I write any word with i before e. Sr. Maura Faulkner, you taught me the joy of both analyzing and creating good writing. I have dreams—literally—of going back to CSB just to take your creative writing class. Zan Chamley and Br. Dietrich Rienhart, I wish you were still around to learn from. I would have loved to be able to share this book with you. Thanks to you, Zan, I still diagram sentences in my head as I write. You taught me the science of grammar. Dietrich, I still imagine your red-pen comments in the margins pushing me to elucidate. You taught me the art of clarity.

In my work world, I have been lucky to have so many wonderful colleagues over the years that have taught me, steered me in the right direction, and supported me—from Extension to Ramsey County to deepSEE: Mary Ann Gwost Hennen, Donna Rae Scheffert, Joyce Jacobs, Jules Laing, Lilliana Espondaburu, Christina Monesterio, Yared Girma, Maria Manske, Aaron Kesher, Amy Batiste, Nehrwr Abdul-Wahid, Phyllis Braxton, Namita Eveloy, Beth Zemske. I have learned from each of you and am grateful for our work together.

Undoubtedly this book is possible primarily because of my clients—thousands of groups that are too many to list, yet each has enriched me in so many ways. Many of my stories to explain the process of Filter Shifting either come from you or have been vetted by you, so my apologies as they won't be new to you. Thank you for giving me the opportunity to work with you to bring theory to practice and prove these concepts. You allowed me to witness the developmental process over and over again, helping me understand the intricacies of how we develop, and showing me courage, vulnerability, and wisdom throughout. You believed in the power of cultural competence, were open to the process, and asked the tough questions that forced me to understand these concepts at a deeper level. Most importantly, you both trusted me and taught me.

Certain client and association partners have supported me for so many years. You have influenced my work, taught me, and inspired me. Thank you for inviting me in to partner with you: Marie Logsden, Marveen Hart, Deborah Foster, Marti Raines, Lisa Fain, Chris Matuseski, Elita Rosillo-Christiansen, Carmilita Tursi, Yusef Mgeni, Sally Baas, Nsombi Ricketts, Kjirsten

Mickesh, Bill Wells, Ghafar Lakanwal, Soina Alvarez-Robinson, and Violet Arnold. I am especially thankful for the continual support from Lynnette Geschwind and Rosemarie Merrigan. You've believed in my work and supported me as a person. I am grateful for your encouragement, your authentic collaboration, and most importantly your friendship.

When it comes to this specific book, the list of those who have contributed in some way is very long.

I could rest easy through this process knowing that I had David Koehser on my team. Thank you, David, for watching out for me and providing a calm reassurance through it all.

Thank you to my instructors from the Loft Literary Center, Mary Carroll and Ashley. Though I know what you passed along to me is only a small fraction of your expertise, it was a treasure of knowledge for me. You were both instructive and kind in your feedback. I am also grateful for all my fellow writers from my Loft courses: Peggy, Cher, William, Marilyn, Amelia, Kim, Jennifer, Peter, Heather, Liza, Lauren, Victor, Mary, Jessica, Janna, Laura, Lia, Christian, Blair, Susan, Grant, Brandon, Nadine, Chester, Sheryl, Carrie, Lloyd, Alia, Lynn, Avital, Cherste, Dave, Candy, Abby, Pat, Mel. Especially my small group in Mary Carroll's class: Sharon, Day, Paula, and Sandra, thank you for your thoughtful feedback and encouragement. You gave me courage and inspiration as I was beginning to write, and for that I am so thankful. I learned from each of you, from your writing, and from all of your breathtaking life experiences.

I am thankful for all of the comfy corners of Caribou coffee shops. Thank you, Caribou baristas, for putting up with me sitting in a corner writing for hours.

Kaylene Weiser, you likely don't realize how you inspire me in so many ways—your courage, your humor, and your endless positivity. It was you mentioning your book club that inspired me to enroll in the Loft courses and actually get started writing.

Jeenee Lee, you made these concepts beautifully and logically come alive graphically, in ways I could have never imagined.

Chris Ayers, I am grateful for your continual guidance, encouragement, and generosity. Thank you for taking me to the authors' conference, introducing me to David, and opening so many doors of opportunity for me.

Thank you to the team at Morgan James. First and foremost, thank you, David Hancock, for believing in me and creating such a fabulous publishing company that actually honors authors by partnering with authenticity and openness. You, Keri Wilson, Tiffany Gibson, and Jim Howard continually brought clarity to the complexity of this process, kindly educating me along the way. Thank you for your patience with and support of me and this work.

To Meg Partridge and Angie Kiesling, you brought clarity and precision to my writing. Thank you for your patience, persistence, and positivity through this process.

Thank you, Donna Rae Scheffert, for being a continual and invaluable role model, friend, and confidant. Encouragement and support are always wonderful to receive, but coming from you those actions give me an added dose of confidence. I've always valued your feedback, and the thoughts you provided to my manuscript were no exception.

Aaron Kesher, aka Mr. Grammar Pants, you more than any other individual have helped me to clarify these concepts and refine and communicate all these ideas rolling around in my head. Through the years of working together you have been an invaluable sounding board and an endless source of fun and positive energy. I very much appreciate your work on my first manuscripts—from big-picture concepts to detailed edits. Knowing I had your help gave me an extra dose of confidence through this process, and for that I am grateful.

Thank you, Keziban Ezzell. While the work with my clients allowed the content of this book to be born, my spiritual work with you helped me bring the light into this writing. You taught me how to let go, trust, and allow the beauty and light into my life and, in turn, into this writing. I am very grateful.

To the Souffront family, thank you for welcoming me into your fold. I am blessed to be a part of such a loving, caring family. Thank you for your daily support and encouragement.

I am so grateful for the family and the circumstances I had the privilege of being born into. To each of my siblings, Maureen Gearino, Beth Strootman, Mary Carole Hornaman, Tim Taylor, Dan Taylor, Kevin Taylor, Kate Johnson, and Ann Schumacher, thank you for your unrelenting support and love. You have been my role models of love, commitment, humor, and hard work. Thank you for setting the bar high through your daily examples.

To my brother John and my parents, Lucille and Jerry Taylor, it brings me comfort to believe you are witness to this work even though you're no longer with us. John, you were a living example of inclusion and taught me so much about what unconditional acceptance looks like. Mom and Dad, I still benefit every day from your quiet strength, selfless generosity, and profound love.

I am so very grateful for the amazing privilege I had to be raised by you.

To my kids, Cora, Ana Elisa, Gabriel, and Miguel, thank you for your patience with me and with this process. You fill my life with joy, laughter, hope, and meaning. I am grateful for each of you and for the light you bring into my life and into the world.

Thank you to my husband, Miguel. It's a beautiful experience to share a life with someone, and I feel so very blessed that you are my someone. I thank the Divine for all the fateful and unpredictable turns that led me to you and brought our two worlds together. You are a never-ending source of strength for me, and I am grateful for your unyielding encouragement, steadfast strength, and tenacious, big heart.

Finally, I thank the Divine for the beauty of life. I am grateful for the circumstances I was born into and for the many opportunities I have been afforded. Thank you for the rich and joyful journey you have created for me. I hope this work is a reflection of your light and love.

A free eBook edition
is available with the
purchase of this book.

To claim your free eBook edition:

1. Download the Shelfie app.
2. Write your name in upper case in the box.
3. Use the Shelfie app to submit a photo.
4. Download your eBook to any device.

Shelfie

A free eBook edition is available
with the purchase of this print book.

CLEARLY PRINT YOUR NAME ABOVE IN UPPER CASE

Instructions to claim your free eBook edition:
1. Download the Shelfie app for Android or iOS
2. Write your name in **UPPER CASE** above
3. Use the Shelfie app to submit a photo
4. Download your eBook to any device

Print & Digital Together Forever.

Snap a photo   Free eBook   Read anywhere

The Morgan James
Speakers Group

↑ www.TheMorganJamesSpeakersGroup.com

We connect Morgan James published authors with live and online events and audiences whom will benefit from their expertise.

CPSIA information can be obtained
at www.ICGtesting.com
Printed in the USA
BVHW05s1704010818
523279BV00001B/19/P

9 781630 479787